THE DANGER ZONE

HOW YOU CAN PROTECT YOURSELF FROM RAPE, ROBBERY, AND ASSAULT

Stay Safe

Til Harma

THE DANGER ZONE

HOW YOU CAN PROTECT YOURSELF FROM RAPE, ROBBERY, AND ASSAULT

by

Patricia Harman

Parkside Publishing
205 W. Touhy Avenue
Park Ridge, Illinois 60068-5881

The Danger Zone

ISBN 0-942421-46-9

Printed in the United States of America

CONTENTS

Dedicated to those who have survived
and those who will survive

A portion of the proceeds from this book are being donated to the Prince William, VA Sexual Assault Victim's Advocacy Service (SAVAS) in recognition of their compassion and support of sexual assault victims.

INTRODUCTION

Most of us have been in the Danger Zone at one time or another in our lives. It is a time or a place where we are vulnerable to violent crime. Violent crime is a fact of life in our society. Small towns and big cities alike have experienced the trauma and destruction violent crime leaves in its wake. If you were attacked, would you know what to do? If you awoke and found someone standing in your bedroom would your reaction trigger violence or prevent it?

There are no magic words of advice that will keep you safe from crime. But if you acknowledge the possibility of crime, you can certainly reduce the odds of being targeted as a victim. And if you are a victim, you will be prepared to know what to do.

The truth is, every crime is different. Every criminal has different motivations and every victim has different limitations. But this doesn't mean you are powerless. You can decrease the chances of being selected as a victim. You can plan so that you will make the right choices if you are attacked. This book is about prevention. Its intent is to teach you to do all you can to keep from becoming a victim. It will also provide you with the knowledge and confidence you need to create a plan that you will design, mentally execute, then store away so it will be there for you should you ever need it. Totally aggressive or passive approaches are not the key here. Rather, survival depends on your honest assessment of your own strengths and weaknesses, and understanding which choices deter violence.

1

APPEARANCES ARE EVERYTHING

You are walking through a dark parking lot to your car. It is late at night and there is no one else around. You think you hear a noise but you can't tell if it came from in front of you or behind you. You look around, but you do not see anyone.

Suddenly you are aware of your own heartbeat. You begin to walk a little faster and breathe a little harder. You think you see a shadow out of the corner of your eye. Your car is still fifty feet away. You reach for your keys and try to pick out the key to your car door. Your hands are shaking. Finally, you reach your car and unlock the door. Quickly, you climb inside, lock the door, and begin to breathe a little easier. You are safe now.

Most of us can think back to a time when we have had a sudden wave of panic or fear. If you have ever been a victim of crime, any crime, your attitudes and behaviors have been forever affected and altered. If you have been fortunate enough never to have been a victim of crime, you may be living under the assumption that it will not happen to you. Logically, you know it is possible, but you are probably not doing everything you could to prevent yourself from being selected as a victim.

The outward appearance you project can determine your chances of becoming a victim. You may think, "Why should I have to change my behavior? The criminals are allowed to roam the streets and do as they please. It doesn't seem fair!" You're right, it's not fair. While you should not and do not have to live behind bars and carry two guns and a switchblade in order to protect yourself, you do have to take responsibility for making choices that will help you stay safe. Awareness and a few personal safety habits can swing the odds greatly in your favor and you won't have to completely alter your lifestyle.

Have you ever stopped to think about how many times you or someone you love has entered the Danger Zone? The Danger Zone is a time and place when you were most vulnerable to a violent attack. You have probably entered this zone more often than you know. What do you think a robber or a rapist looks for in a victim? One thing is certain, rapists do not just get up in the morning and go out the front door and grab the first person they see. Most violent crime, particularly rape, is premeditated in some manner.

Location is often the first consideration. Remember, criminals have a lot on the line. If they choose the wrong person, the wrong location, or the wrong time, they may end up in jail. They don't set up an elaborate surveillance, of course. Most criminals are not rocket scientists, but they know the best time and location to commit their crime. They also know, even if only unconsciously, what to look for in a victim.

Have you ever gone people watching? You can really get an insight into personal safety just by watching others. The next time you are in a shopping mall, take a look around and see if you can pick out a "potential victim" attitude. I do not mean to suggest that some people "ask for it." No one asks to be a victim of crime. But some folks are unwittingly signalling that they would be an easy target.

The Eyes Have It

Direct eye contact can be a deterrent to violent crime for many reasons. The habit of making direct eye contact with people sends a message of confidence. This particular habit will be harder for some than for others, but it is important to your personal safety. If you are uncomfortable with direct eye contact among your peers, your family, or at social gatherings, you do not have to change your basic personality. Try a casual, brief period of eye contact that says, "I am aware that you are looking at me." What you are displaying is the appearance of an aggressive personality.

If you are walking in public and you are aware that others are looking at you, try looking back. I don't mean an offensive or antagonistic glare, but simply brief eye contact. They may be perfectly harmless. Perhaps they are admiring your outfit. You may look like someone they know, or maybe they are just people-watching. Whatever the motivation, the message from you is clear:"I am aware that you are looking at me."

Is this a deterrent to violent crime? You bet it is. The majority of criminals are looking for an easy target. For the criminal, this means the least amount of resistance and the smallest risk of detection or identification. With so many potential victims available, would they still take a chance on you? The odds are against it.

Are the Brain and Body Functioning Together?

Is the body on automatic pilot while the brain is somewhere else? Criminals watch for this. You may be able to recall many times when you have not been aware of your surroundings as you went somewhere—your mind was "someplace else." You spent that time getting from Point A to Point B thinking about what you had to do once you got there. This is a dangerously careless habit you can easily correct. One of your best personal safety safeguards is conscious awareness of your environment: living in the moment you are in, not in the future or the past.

For instance, you are going to the grocery store. You have parked your car and are walking through the parking lot, but you are not thinking about what lies between you and the store. You are probably making your shopping list. "I need milk, bread crumbs, and the dog is almost out of food. Do I have my checkbook?" Your preoccupation is probably evident from your outward appearance. Your body is going through the motions of walking through the parking lot, but your brain is already in the store. If someone is out there waiting for a target, they are probably looking at you.

When you are going from your home to your car or your car to a store, keep your wits closely about you. Concentrate on the path you are taking. Think about where you are going and scan the area that separates you from your destination. You will want to keep your head up so you can use eye contact if necessary. Walk with a quick confident step. Tune out the many responsibilities and priorities in your life. Your immediate priority is to get there safely. Stay alert. If you are not alert, you will not be able to identify a potential danger zone. If you cannot identify it, you cannot avoid it.

Keys

Keep your home or car key in your hand and ready to use ahead of time. Should someone run at you from across a parking lot, or come walking toward you from around a corner, you may have only a split second to put that key into the lock and get to safety. If you have to reach into your purse or fumble with several keys, you may not make it in time.

My mother lived in Trenton, New Jersey for a few years and she had this key technique down to a science. When she got home from work, she would park her car, get her key ready, then scan the street. If there were no visible hazards, she would get out of the car, walk up the stairs, and be in the house in under five seconds. She was not paranoid or fearful every time she came home; she had grown up in this neighborhood and was familiar and comfortable with her surroundings. But if she ever found herself confronted with a

4

threat, she was safe in the knowledge that she had practiced getting to the safety of her home quickly. It was a good habit.

You will find that, after a few days of making yourself go through the trouble of getting the key out and ready, it will become second nature to you.

Instincts

Your instincts are a powerful weapon in the prevention of violent crime. Time after time, victims of crime who were fortunate enough to live through an attack have made statements like "I saw him before it happened and he gave me the willies," or, "I knew something was wrong the minute I walked into my apartment," or, "All night I had the creeps," or, "Something just didn't feel right about that place."

Try to remember a time when your instincts were talking to you. Think back to some time in your life when everything was going along just fine when you suddenly became nervous for no apparent reason. Some people refer to this as "the bells going off" or "the willies." Our own instincts are vital to our protection. Trust them.

Your instincts may tell you to take an umbrella when there is not a cloud in the sky, or to call a friend who may need you. Practice tuning in to your instincts. If you get a gut feeling to avoid a situation or person, follow it. What do you have to lose? By conditioning yourself to listen to those gut reactions you will be better prepared to react appropriately in a dangerous situation.

Sometimes it may appear that your instincts were falsely triggered. You felt apprehensive as you were walking to your car but nothing happened, so you wrote it off as foolishness. In fact, you don't know for sure that you weren't in danger, do you? Maybe someone was watching. Maybe there was a danger that never revealed itself. More often than not, if you are feeling uneasy, there is a reason for it.

Examine Your Lifestyle

Evaluate your lifestyle and assess whether or not there are

changes you can make to enhance your personal safety. Single people tend to be victims of crime more often than those who are not. While it is certainly not necessary for you to get married, it is important to realize that you are in a higher risk group. More awareness can decrease your chances of being a victim of violent crime.

Are you in the habit of using the stairs instead of the elevator? While this may be a desirable physical fitness habit, it is not a good personal safety habit. Do you leave work late at night? Do you walk to the parking lot alone? Perhaps you take an evening class at a university. Be able to identify danger zones in your life. What can you do to minimize them?

Your outward appearance may deter violent crime, yet this does not completely eliminate the possibility. There may come a time when you are simply in the wrong place at the wrong time. This does not make it your fault. Even if you make a mistake and use poor judgment, it is not your fault if you are selected as a victim. You owe it to yourself to do as much as possible to protect yourself from violent crime.

Review

1. Practice keeping your head up and making eye contact with people who make eye contact with you.

2. Keep your wits about you and your head clear of other thoughts when you are at the peak of vulnerability. In most cases, this is when you are walking from one place to another.

3. Have the door key in your hand before you approach the entrance. Do not wait until you are at the door to look for the key.

4. Trust your instincts. If you feel like something may be wrong, it probably is.

5. Examine your lifestyle and see where some changes can be made to enhance your overall personal safety.

2
THE PLAN

In spite of all your best efforts, you may still become the target of a violent crime. This chapter will help you design a personal plan of action. It must be tailored to you, as only you know what your limitations and capabilities are. Before you can do this you must first be able to identify potential hazards so you can avoid them.

Environmental Hazards

Environmental hazards may include poor lighting, reduced visibility, wooded areas, and the like. Time of day is also an important factor. Nighttime hours are particularly hazardous because of limited visibility and the absence of other people. Are you leaving work at five o'clock along with one hundred other employees in your building? Or are you leaving at seven-thirty because you have some extra work? You should adjust your behavior accordingly. You can do this by being more wary as it gets later in the evening. Ask a coworker for an escort to your car. If possible, take work home with you in order to leave earlier with the crowd.

Areas of concealment are important to be aware of. When

parking your car, choose a spot in the center of the lot where there are other cars and people around. Make sure you park where there is adequate lighting. If you are parking while there is still daylight but you intend to leave after dark, look for the street light and park underneath it.

Environmental hazards are encountered every day and in many cases cannot be avoided. Your best protection is to identify a potential problem and be aware of the possibility that it could become a danger zone. Once you have done this you will be in a better frame of mind to deal with a problem, should it arise.

Potential Suspects

Not all criminals look like criminals. Ask yourself, does this person belong here? You see a man standing outside a women's restroom, but the men's restroom is located at the other end of the building. Does this man belong here? Maybe he is waiting for his wife or girlfriend, maybe not. You see a woman you don't recognize on your office floor, or in an employees-only area. Does this woman belong here? You see someone new in the laundry room of your apartment complex, someone that you have never seen in the building. Does this person belong here? You get the idea.

Notice how the person is dressed. If it is eighty degrees outside and someone is standing in the back of a convenience store wearing a winter coat, get out of there fast or you may find yourself in the middle of a robbery. Go to a safe location and call the police to report the incident.

Observe the behavior of other people. If they are doing something unusual or trying to conceal themselves in any way, it could mean trouble. Evaluate how close someone is to you and whether or not you can get to safety before he or she can get to you. Notice if anyone is approaching you. Many attacks begin with an initial non-threatening contact. "Hold up a minute! May I ask you a question?" or, "Do you have the time?" Keep moving. Listen to what your instincts are telling you.

Most criminals rely on surprise when executing a crime. Take that element of surprise away. When you identify hazards and react accordingly, you just may deter the attack altogether.

Alternatives

The advantage in being able to identify a threat is that you can take steps to avoid it. One way of dealing with a threat is to wait it out. This is a tough one for most of us because we are always in a hurry, but it is one of the most practical options.

If there is someone in the parking lot or the hallway and you are apprehensive, wait until he or she goes away, or wait for other people. There is safety in numbers. You don't have to be in the company of friends to use them for safety. If you are coming out of a store and there is a person that you will have to walk past who is making you nervous, wait. In very short order, a woman and her three screaming children may well be walking to that same parking lot. Walk out at the same time. Two adults and three screaming children are not an enticing scene for a robber or a rapist. Leaving a late class? Walk out with your classmates. In most cases criminals are looking for someone who is alone. Other people are your best protection.

Another option might be to ask for an escort. Ask the security person, store manager, or parking lot attendant to walk with you. You could also phone the police. If you do not have access to a phone, you may want to ask someone to phone the police for you. If you live in a large city, the police may not be able to respond quickly to a call about a suspicious person—they may have more urgent priorities. But your safety is urgent to you and it can't hurt to call if you have no other alternative.

Your Plan

What if you do not see an attack coming? This is where your personal plan of action comes into play. It is vital to think about an attack before it happens. You don't want to waste precious time as your mind cycles through panic, shock, and disbelief. Remember, the criminal has a plan. His adrenalin is pumping, he has advanced to the confrontational stage of his plan, and he is committed. To survive, you have to be equally committed.

Every year people are killed or injured seriously as a result of violent crimes. Here's why:

1. They failed to anticipate the danger.

2. They panicked and were unable to do anything to help themselves.

3. They failed to use proper defense tactics.

4. They gave up.

You can prepare yourself for an attack. You can survive. In a situation where you have no control, your survival plan may be your lifeline.

The first step is to try not to panic. You are going to be scared, but do not lose control. You must keep a clear head and your wits about you.

The second step is a split-second assessment of your environment. Is help available? If you scream, is it likely that anyone will hear you? If not, don't waste the energy. Is there an escape route? Does your assailant have a weapon?

The steps that follow will be entirely up to you and your own physical and psychological limitations. You must be flexible because your first plan may not be effective and you will have to rely on a back-up plan. Without a plan you will panic. You must prepare yourself mentally today so that your brain will know what to do later.

Review

1. Environmental Hazards

   –Hour of the day.

   –Busy or deserted.

   –Hiding places.

   –Adequate lighting.

2. Potential Suspects

   –Do they belong there?

   –How are they dressed or behaving?

3. Alternatives to Confronting a Threat

   –Wait until they leave.

   –Wait for other people.

   –Ask for an escort.

   –Notify police.

4. Your Plan

   –Stay calm and keep a clear head.

   –Assess the environment, look for help.

   –Is there a weapon?

   –Evaluate your personal limitations.

   –Objective is survival.

   –Formulate a plan now; later may be too late.

3

ROBBERY

A robbery is the taking of property or money from a person by the use of force, threats, or intimidation. Many people confuse robbery with larceny (stealing a car from a parking lot) and burglary (breaking into a home and taking belongings without the owner's knowledge). In larceny and burglary, the property is taken from a home or place. In robbery, property is taken directly from the victim. The victim is physically involved in the crime. Robbery is often accompanied by assault, and sometimes death.

Here is where your plan comes into play. Decide right now that your life is more important than any property you have. Your life is more important than your wallet, more important than your purse, more important than your car. Make those decisions a part of your plan, or your anger may override common sense. When angry, you may find yourself fighting for that property. Maybe you will get it back, or maybe you will die trying. Let's review some specific robbery scenarios.

Purse Snatching

We've gone through many different strategies regarding

how to carry a purse. At one time we advised women to place the strap over their shoulder and across their chest, wrapping the band around the wrist, to help them hold on to the purse should someone grab it. But what happens is that the victim gets dragged down the street a half a block or so before the strap breaks or she gets so banged up she has to let go and the criminal gets the purse anyway.

A better idea is to simply let it go. Yes, let go of your purse. Keep it close to your body and low in profile, but be able to release it if necessary.

In one case, a woman was followed home from a neighborhood park. She was in her car in the middle of the afternoon. She had two small children with her and lived in a very nice, very quiet subdivision. The man who had been following her parked his car down the street from her driveway and began to approach on foot. She saw him before she exited the vehicle and did not recognize him from the neighborhood. It seemed odd to her, the bells were gently starting to ring, but she was not listening. She got her two small children out of the car and walked to the front porch. As she was searching for her keys, he ran toward her from across the lawn. She was unable to get the key out in time to get into the house. He grabbed her purse and tried to take it. With her two small children cowering behind her she took a firm hold on the purse and got into a tug-of-war with the robber. It didn't last long. He punched her in the face and she landed in the bushes. He grabbed the purse and was gone. "I'm not the kind of person that would fight back like that," she said. "I don't know what came over me." The police knew. Anger had won out over fear. What right did this man have to come onto her front porch and take her purse? In a split second, she thought of the credit card companies she would have to deal with and the lines at the Division of Motor Vehicles she would have to stand in to replace her license.

Is it unusual that she would be thinking of her drivers license in the middle of an attack? Not at all. If your brain is not prepared for an attack scenario it will retreat to what is

13

normal. Surprising thoughts and emotions go through your mind in a moment of panic. That is why you must train yourself to concentrate on survival in an attack situation. Your plan is vital to your survival. The plan is, if someone tries to take your money—your purse or your wallet—you will let it go. You will be angry, but you will be alive.

In the days of crack cocaine, PCP, and all of the other mind-altering drugs out there, a robber may be willing to kill you for the contents of your purse or pocket.

Think about an area near where you live where you might be susceptible to a mugging. Go through the entire scenario in your head. Imagine yourself walking alone. Suddenly you hear footsteps behind you, someone slams into you. Your purse is snatched from your hand, or your wallet is pulled from your pocket. You let it go; you do not resist. You go the opposite direction of the robber, walking quickly to safety, and phone the police. While you are waiting for the police, you try to remember as much as you can. When the police arrive, they take the information about the attack. Afterwards you go home to your family and tell them what happened. This is the best you can do.The alternative could be so much worse for you and your family.

Street Robbery

You must remember that robbers are dangerous, violent, and unpredictable.They are often very nervous or under the influence of alcohol or other drugs.It will be unlikely that you will have the time to size the robber up and decide if you can win physically. There are those who have successfully fought back and saved their property. But there are many more who fight back and are maimed or killed. People die for wallets, purses, and personal belongings. Your property for your life is not a fair trade. The press often glorifies people who fight back in a robbery. You have seen the headlines: "WOMAN BEATS MUGGER WITH UMBRELLA, SAVES SOCIAL SECURITY CHECK." Three days later on the fifth page you'll find, "WOMAN DIES FROM STAB WOUNDS AFTER

STRUGGLE WITH MUGGER."

While some robbers are predisposed to violence, others are not. There have been many recorded cases of accidental shootings in robberies. A robber got nervous because someone made a sudden move. It is doubtful that most robbers set out with intent to kill. If that was their intention, why would they go through the trouble of holding you up? Why not just kill you, drag you into an alley, and take what they want? What robbers want is your money, your property, and your cooperation. Many robberies have escalated to murders because people tried to fight back, refused to meet the demands of the robber, or made a sudden move that alarmed the robber. Cooperation is the best way to handle a robber and come out alive.

Remember your plan. Stay in control. Take a breath and look around. Do what you are told and make no sudden moves. Try to remember what you can about the robber but do not make it appear that you are studying the person. Keep your priorities in line. You and your loved ones come first, then your property.

Now I want you to experience a robbery. More and more, in training circles, instructors are focusing on the benefits of mental preparation for high stress situations. This is one of the best ways to prepare yourself for an emergency. Live it in your head. Go through the entire scenario step by step. You may even want to close your eyes and practice deep breathing while you walk yourself through it. In an emergency your brain will recall that training and get you through the crisis.

For your practice scenarios, it is always best to visualize a location that you frequent often. You are walking out of your office building, a local bar, or maybe past an alley in your neighborhood. Someone pushes you against a car and says, "I have a gun. Hand me your wallet and don't turn around." Think about slowly reaching for your wallet. Imagine yourself taking a breath and looking around to see if there is any help available. Your heart will be pounding and your hands will be shaking but you will get the wallet out and hand it

15

over. "What else have you got?" the robber asks. You say you have a watch, for it would be foolish to lie about something that is in plain view. You are ordered to remove it, which you do. The robber harshly pushes your head down and tells you to stay put. You do. After the robber has gone, you go to the closest safe location available and call the police.

Should a robber get your identification and keys, you should have the locks changed on your home and car immediately. In all likelihood your wallet or purse will be discarded by the robber after the money and credit cards have been removed, but it is best not to take chances. In addition to having your locks changed, you should be very aware of any suspicious people in the days and weeks that follow. Don't hesitate to contact police if you notice a suspicious person around your property or if you feel you are being followed.

Everyone's plan of action will be different based on their own assessment of the situation and their limitations, but do not wait until a robbery happens. Visualize it now. If you formulate a plan now and it happens later, you are less likely to panic. You will still be scared, but your brain will say, "Okay, we've talked about this before. This is not completely new. The first thing I am going to do is . . . " Prepare yourself now. There will be no time later.

Automatic Teller Machines

Law enforcement agencies are encouraging the banking industry to design automatic teller machines more safely. By placing them in open parking lots or drive-through window lanes, the machines can be used in relative safety. Some banks have done this, some have not. You may want to consider this information when you decide where to bank. You want your money to be safe; it only stands to reason that you should expect to be safe when you are withdrawing or depositing your money. Walk-up teller machines can also be dangerous. If you were a robber, would you grab a purse for the ten dollars that might be in it, or would you rob someone at an automatic teller machine where the victim could be ordered to withdraw three hundred and fifty dollars? It is a low risk, high take score for the robber. Robbers are well aware of the advantages that walk-up teller machines provide.

These robberies are happening everywhere. If you must use these machines, try to use them during daylight and try to have someone else with you. If you decide to use them at night, take a ride or a good look around the area first to make sure there is no one suspicious hanging around. If something does not look or feel right, go to another location. If someone is standing alone at the machine, wait until that person leaves before you approach. That person may be filling out a deposit slip, or may be waiting to rob you.

Review

1. Purse Snatching

    –Listen to your instincts.

    –Keep your purse close to your body and low in profile.

    –If a robber tries to take it, do not fight. Let it go.

    –Visualize the attack and formulate your plan. The ending is always the same. You go home when it's over.

2. Robbery/Mugging

    –Cooperate and make no sudden moves or statements.

    –Formulate a plan. Go through a robbery step by step in your mind.

3. Automatic Tellers

    –Try to use banks with drive up automatic tellers.

    –Look around the area first. If anything is suspicious, go to another machine.

    –Do not use after dark.

17

4
SAFE AT HOME

Your own home is where you feel most secure. Familiarity, family, and personal possessions all work together to make you feel safe and shielded from the outside world. But if the outside world decided to drop in, would your home be an easy target? It is good to feel safe in your home, but it is not safe just because it is "home." A false sense of security can jeopardize your personal safety. While no home is completely intruder-proof, you can make your home intruder-resistant. Hardware as well as safety practices should be included in your home security plan.

Hardware

Have you ever been locked out of your home and been able to get in without breaking glass? If the answer is yes, you have a security problem. You are not an intruder, you are a home owner. You probably did not even use a tool to gain entry. If you can get in, so can the most inexperienced burglar.

You do not have to build a fortress or spend thousands of dollars on an alarm system to improve your security. Professional burglars can be extremely cunning and they are difficult to deter, but most home intruders do not plan or use sophisticated entry tools. Most are opportunists and carry little more than a six-inch screwdriver or a crowbar. In fact, many intruders do not carry a tool at all. They find everything they need to break in by looking through the open garage or tool shed. In many cases they just keep turning doorknobs until they find one that has been left unlocked. The first rule of physical security is to use the hardware you have available to you. Locks will not keep an intruder out if you do not use them.

Home Security

Let me walk you through a typical home and point out physical security flaws. We will be looking at this home in very much the same way as an intruder would look at your home.

The front view of the home reflects a well-maintained yard and house. The lawn is neatly trimmed and free of debris and the home has a cared-for appearance. The shrubbery is low and trimmed away from all doors and windows.This is a plus. Neatly kept neighborhoods are a deterrent to crime.

The house numbers are posted over the front door, but they are gold-plated script and difficult to read. Plain block numbers, colored to contrast with the house color are easier for police and firemen to locate in case of an emergency.

The homeowners here have a wooden sign hanging from the porch with the family name on it. Advertising the family name encourages the intruder to phone ahead to see if the family is home or to pose as a marketing surveyor asking questions about your family. The family name is used to convince you the survey is legitimate.

The front door is made of solid wood construction. A hollow door is not a safe door. There is a deadbolt lock on the door. This is an absolute must.A spring latch lock (a locking doorknob) will not keep an intruder out. Because you can see the lock from the outside, intruders can tell what they are up against just by looking at your front door. A spring latch lock will be chosen by an intruder more often than a deadbolt.

This home has a good solid door and a good lock, but as we look at the door frame we find a problem. One of the most overlooked areas in entry door security is the strike plate. The strike plate is the metal square mounted on the door frame. The bolt, when in the locked position, fits into this square.The problem is that this strike plate is secured to the door frame by two half-inch screws. If someone put a sturdy shoulder to the door, the door and the lock would hold up just fine, but the little half-inch screws would give way, the door frame would break under the stress and the door would come open. Replacing these half-inch screws with three-inch screws or a reinforced strike plate will make the doors to your home more resistant to intruders.

There is no viewer or peep hole on this door. The home owner needs some way to identify who is on the other side of that door before opening it. There is a door chain mounted on the inside of the door. Talking to a stranger through a chain is not safe. It will probably not even slow down an intruder. In fact, by assuming that the chain will provide you with security you are more likely to open the door to an intruder. This may provide all the leverage he needs to break the door open. It is much easier to break through an open door with a chain than it is to break down a door secured with a dead bolt lock. If you have a chain, use it, but use it only for additional security and not as a protective barrier when dealing with a stranger at your door.

Let's take a look at the sliding glass doors. To intruders, a sliding glass door means easy access. This homeowner has added to the sliding glass door security by making three inexpensive upgrades. First, a secondary patio door lock was added. Next, a broom stick was placed in the interior track to jam the door should someone try to open it from the outside. Last, the dead space that allows the door to be lifted off of its track was eliminated. If you open a sliding door halfway and lift up on it, in most cases you will find that the door will lift right off its track. To keep this from happening, open the door completely and place a thin piece of wood in the upper channel of the door track. This will eliminate the dead space. Now when someone lifts up on the door, it bumps against the wood in the track and will not lift off the track. With these three upgrades, sliding glass doors are very difficult to penetrate short of coming through the glass. But breaking glass is noisy and intruders don't like noise.

The windows are double sash windows with wooden frames. They are secured with a crescent lock. Additional security for these windows is as close as a household drill. With the window in the closed and locked position, drill a hole through the corner of the first sash and halfway through the second sash.This should be done on both corners of the window. Then place a half-inch eyebolt in the holes. The eyebolt should slide in and out easily for quick removal in case of an emergency. Do not ever nail your windows shut.

The hardware features listed above may not apply to every home, but there are other resources available. Many police departments will send out an officer to walk through your home with you and point out security flaws. They also may have literature that can help you with your home security assessment.Some bonded locksmiths will give you a free home security check in the hope that you will hire them to make the upgrades. Hardware store owners or managers can also help. There are also publications at your local library on proper home security. Make sure that the home security upgrades you make are not in conflict with your local fire safety codes. A phone call to your local fire marshall can insure that you are within fire safety regulations.

A Stranger at Your Door

What if there is a stranger at your door? The person may have a perfectly legitimate reason for being there, but how will you be able to tell? You start by not opening your door. We've been conditioned to open the door when we hear a knock and most of us do not even think about how vulnerable we become when we unlatch that lock and turn the knob. Identify the person on the outside by talking with him or her through the door and checking credentials through the viewer. If you are satisfied with the credentials and you wish to do business, it is your choice. Remember to listen to your instincts.

Generally, you should not do business of any kind if it requires letting a stranger into your home, particularly when you are alone. Don't be intimidated by a hard sell or an aggressive person who insists that you open the door to speak. Don't do anything that makes you uncomfortable. If you don't want to deal with this person, you don't have to. Ask the stranger to leave. If the person stays at your door, say you are calling the police, then make the call. Remember, sometimes it is okay to be rude. Don't sacrifice your safety for the sake of good manners.

What if it appears to be an emergency? A young woman comes to your home and pounds on your door saying there has been an accident and she needs to come in and call an ambulance. This is a judgment call. Did you hear an accident? Can you see one? The best way to handle this situation would be to call an ambulance for her. Tell her you have made the call and that the ambulance is on its way to your address and she should wait outside and flag it down.

If someone comes to your house requesting help you will certainly want to do whatever you can. Make a quick assessment of the situation before opening the door. Listen to what the person is saying. Listen to what your instincts are telling you.

Immediately pick up the phone and dial the emergency number in your area. Tell the dispatcher you need assistance and give your address along with information you have, regardless of how minimal it might be. Emergency services personnel will then be on their way.

If it was a set-up, you will not be alone for long. If it was not, you have wasted no time in getting this person the help that is needed.

When the Stranger Has Been Invited

You have to call a repairman to your home and you are there alone. Are you safe? In most cases it is an honest tradesman on a service call. But there is always that slight chance that the person is also a rapist or a thief in a job that offers easy access to homes and women alone. It has happened; it will happen again. When you need a serviceman, you don't simply have to take the risk. Exercise your options and reduce your chances of becoming a victim.

Have Someone With You. Arrange to have someone with you —a friend, a neighbor, or a relative. You don't need to hire a security guard to stand watch, or invite a friend who just happens to be packing a gun. There is safety in numbers. Your friend is not there to physically protect you but to swing the odds in your favor. Two people are much more of a risk for the criminal than one alone.

Talk On The Phone. You can plan to be on the phone with a friend when the service person arrives. Put the phone down long enough to let him in, show him the washer or television set, and tell him you have someone on the phone. Remain on the phone throughout the service call and simply put the phone down if you need to speak with the service person or write a check. You will have to ask some patience of your friend on the phone, but maybe you can return the favor sometime. An attack is less likely with the possibility of someone on the other end of the phone monitoring the situation.

Pretend Someone Is With You. After you have checked the service person's credentials and let him in, yell upstairs or down the hall, "Honey, the repairman is here. I'm going to take him to the laundry room." While he is looking at the machine, you might say, "Excuse me, I'll have to get a check from my husband." You may be uncomfortable leaving this person alone in a room in your home while you talk on the phone or pretend to speak with another person in the house, but, personal possessions can be replaced. It's easy to choose between having your television set taken because you weren't watching his every move and being raped because he

23

thinks you are home alone.

Personal safety practices can be an inconvenience, but how often do you have to call a service person? If the service person is unexpected—like a phone repairman saying he has to come in and check the lines, someone from the gas or electric company, or even a plainclothes police officer—check credentials through your door viewer and ask for a phone number you can call to verify the person's identity. A business office or supervisor can usually be contacted for a quick verification. If he is the real thing, he'll wait. If not, watch him run! Then call the police to report the incident. The next person he tries to fool may not be as safety conscious as you.

Prowlers

A prowler could be a Peeping Tom, someone using your yard as a shortcut, or someone contemplating a burglary. You should handle all of them the same way: call the police. You should not investigate a prowler yourself, nor should any member of your family.

If the sound that you heard is not a normal noise for your house—glass breaking, wood splintering, a thud—get your family together and go to the room in your home that has a telephone and is farthest away from the detected intrusion. Most often this will be a bedroom or den. If you can escape the home altogether, do so. If you are home alone and cannot escape, you may want to make some noise and try to convince the prowler that you have heard the noise and that you have mistaken him for another member of the household. Try yelling, "Hey, John! You've been watching TV all night. Aren't you ever coming to bed?" All the while you are moving to the phone. If the intruder has come to burglarize, he will not want to be seen and may go out the way he came. Call the police. After reporting that you believe you have a prowler, ask the dispatcher to remain on the line with you until the officer arrives. This is a common practice for most police agencies in cases of emergency. If it turns out to be an animal or the police are unable to locate an intruder, there will not be a problem. The area will be checked and you will feel better. If there was a prowler, the presence of police cars have probably sent him on his way.

Motion detection lights are a good deterrent to this type of activity. They are relatively inexpensive and activate only when motion is detected. If a prowler activates the lights, they will not know whether the light is operating on a sensor or the homeowner has turned them on.

Dogs are also a good deterrent. Many burglars would much rather come face-to-face with a homeowner than a dog. You cannot intimidate Spike as easily as you can a person. Unfortunately, some people train their dogs to not bark. Encourage your dog's behavior when he is protecting his home. Say "Good boy" or "Is that a bad man out there, Spike?" This praise will not make Spike a man-eating beast, but it will encourage him to sound off whenever his home is being approached by an outsider. You couldn't ask for a more reliable alarm system. But Spike won't do you any good if you keep him locked in the basement.

Nighttime Burglars

Needless to say, nighttime burglars are extremely dangerous people. At two o'clock in the morning they have a pretty good idea that there are people in the home sleeping. To some degree they expect a confrontation and they are usually prepared to deal with one. Don't confront a nighttime burglar in an attempt to save your property. If he leaves without harming or raping anyone in your family you should consider yourself fortunate. Close the door behind him and phone the police.

If you do not have a plan to this effect, you may try to stop the burglar. Worse, you may actually pursue him. I have heard of housewives chasing burglars for blocks. They did not know what they were going to do if they caught the burglar; they were simply outraged that someone would try to take their stuff. The instinct to fight for what was rightfully theirs took over, and common sense and personal safety went out the window.

You have no idea what you are going to come up against when you decide to confront a nighttime burglar. Families have watched fathers die in their own living rooms trying to stop an intruder from taking property. Remember, the burglar has a plan too. His plan, if you are lucky, may be to run if detected. But his plan could also be to shoot if confronted.

Many homeowners do not detect the burglar until they see him standing in their bedroom. This happens more often than you might think. Burglars know that the master bedroom usually contains a wallet, a purse, and a jewelry box. They might be desperate or brazen enough to try to take one or two things without waking the occupants.

The best advice I can offer here is to stay asleep. Sleep will be difficult to fake when your heart is beating through the covers and a scream is caught in your throat. But if burglars are there to steal, they will want you to stay asleep. They will take the property they have come for and leave.

If you sit up and scream, they will activate their plan. Maybe the plan will be to turn and run or maybe a burglary will turn into a rape or homicide. You can always react with a back-up plan if the need arises, but if you start out by screaming or turning on a light, you may be closing all other avenues of safety. Try to fake sleep and wait for the burglar to leave.

Guns

Purchasing a gun for home safety is relatively easy in most states. But buying one, bringing it home, and placing it in your nightstand for "peace of mind" is irresponsible and dangerous. If you are going to buy one or already have one, learn how to use it. Practice at a firing range, not once, but regularly. When you are transporting it, be sure it's unloaded and locked in the trunk. Get some instruction on how to clean it and always treat it as if it were loaded no matter how many times you've checked to see that it is not. "Unloaded" guns have wounded and killed many gun owners. Do not put the gun in your spouse's hands and say "Here is the safety and here is the trigger. If anyone ever breaks in and I'm not here, this is how it shoots." Anyone who is not trained and is not comfortable with a gun will not be able to use it for self defense. In fact, they are more likely to have it taken away from them by the intruder, who will probably not have any reservations about using it.

For safe storage in the home, a gun should be in one location and the ammunition in another. If the gun is kept loaded and at your bedside, you may be placing innocent people in jeopardy. Suppose you and your family leave for work and school and a seventeen-year-old burglar climbs over your back fence and breaks into your home. He finds the gun in your nightstand. Your neighbor witnesses the break-in and calls the police. The police are responding to what started as a seventeen-year-old with a six-inch screwdriver. Now they are responding to a burglary involving a seventeen-year-old with a loaded gun.

If the safety of the police is not reason enough for you to store the gun properly, then consider the safety of children who are in the home. No matter how mature you think your children might be, no matter how carefully you have explained the weapon and the dangers of handling it, it might not keep their curiosity from getting the best of them. There could be no greater loss than losing a child to a handgun you put within reach. Even if you do not have a gun, you should still discuss gun safety with your children. Perhaps a playmate down the street knows where Dad hides his handgun. When your children see a handgun that comes from any place but you or a toy box, they should treat it like a poisonous snake and run for their lives. Tell them not to look at it, not to touch it, not to discuss it. Just run home as fast as they can and tell an adult.

It is normal to want to protect your home and family, but do not let this sense of duty cloud your common sense. The courts have made it very clear that in order to shoot an intruder in your home or on your property, you must be "in fear of your life." Fear of having your VCR stolen doesn't count. Being angry because an intruder has come onto your property doesn't count. You must feel that this intruder is about to seriously injure or kill you or someone in your family. You should not be the aggressor. If you hear a noise that indicates someone may be breaking in, and then you leave the safety of your bedroom, come down the stairs, open the front door and shoot, it will be difficult to explain how this person was coming after you. If there is an intruder in your home, get your family together and retreat. If the intruder comes after you and you feel your lives are in jeopardy, then it is time for deadly force if you have the means and the mental preparation to handle it.

Keep in mind that law enforcement officers die every year because they hesitate to pull the trigger. With all the training, authority, and justification to take a life when they are in danger of losing their own, they still hesitate. Police officers, homeowners, and people in general place a high value on life —anyone's life. Firing a gun at someone may not be as easy as you think. Your body may be willing but your mind may lock up on you. If you bring out a weapon, and are unable to use it, you may lose it to your attacker.

If your plan involves a firearm or other weapon, visualize yourself using it and pay attention to your reactions. Think about pointing a gun at another human being and looking into his eyes. Think about pulling the trigger and seeing the muzzle flash, smelling the smoke from the gun. Think about watching the bullet enter this person, and watching him fall. Imagine the blood that begins to spread from the body. Think about that kitchen knife you keep under your pillow. Think about how much force you will have to use to stab someone with it, and how close you will have to get to the intruder to use it effectively.

Yes, these scenes are graphic, but consider the facts before you incorporate a deadly weapon into your plan. If you can't walk yourself through it now, you probably will not be able to use your weapon effectively then. You need another plan—a plan that you will feel comfortable executing.

If you decide to use a gun, make sure that you can see the person's eyes before you take any action. If you are shooting at a silhouette, you may be about to kill someone you love. It happens all the time—a husband coming home early from a business trip, a college student home early to surprise the family, a neighbor who found your door blown open by the wind coming in to see if everything is okay. If you can't see the intruder's face, hold your fire.

Coming Home to a Burglarized Home

When you come home to a burglarized home, you won't usually find anything initially to indicate you've been burglarized, since most often a side or rear entry has been used. You may feel a little strange. People are very instinctive about their homes, and you may feel something is not right even before you realize what's happened. You move into the living room and find a bare spot where the VCR used to be. Then it hits you—you've been burglarized. You run to the phone and call the police. "Someone broke into my house!" you say. "I need a police officer here right away!" The dispatcher asks, "Where are you now?," and you reply, "I'm in my kitchen!" The dispatcher asks, "Are you sure the burglar has gone?" and you get a sick feeling in your stomach. Did you miss the burglar by five hours or five minutes? Or did you miss him at all? Maybe he is standing behind the kitchen door or in a closet upstairs.

People become so overwhelmed by the fact that they have been burglarized that they don't consider the possibility that they may have walked into the middle of the crime. If you come home and find you have been burglarized, get out of the house. Do not call your spouse, a neighbor, or even the police. Do not look to see what is missing. Get to safety, then call the police. Make sure they know the house has not been checked and that there is a possibility that the burglar is still inside. Wait for the police to respond.Under these circumstances, their response should be swift. Do not enter the home until they have checked it thoroughly. If you call to report a burglary that has occurred "sometime today," your call will be prioritized as routine. This does not mean your burglary is not important to the police, it is. It simply means that emergency calls involving an immediate threat to life or property will be handled first. You may wait fifteen minutes to several hours depending on the emergency calls that are pending at the time. A burglary in which the homeowner has not checked the house and is standing by outside is not a routine call. It is given much higher priority and will be handled as swiftly as possible. Though guidelines vary from agency to agency, call priorities are relatively standard. Make sure you provide the police dispatcher with enough information to prioritize your call properly.

Review
Hardware

1. Locks cannot help you if you do not use them.

   –Do not leave ground floor windows open.

   –Contact local law enforcement for home security survey.

   –Obtain literature on hardware specifications from Police, library or locksmith.

2. A stranger at your door

   –Do not open or unlock door.

   –Ask for credentials and verify phone number.

3. Servicemen

   –Arrange to have someone home with you.

   –Keep someone on the phone throughout service visit.

   –Pretend that you are not alone.

4. Prowlers

   –Do not investigate, call police.

   –Use motion detection lights.

   –Dogs; do not discourage barking at outsiders.

5. Nighttime Burglars

   –Do not confront.

   –Do not pursue.

6. Guns

   –Obtain proper training.

   –Always treat as if loaded.

   –Store ammunition and gun separately.

   –Instruct children about gun safety.

   –Be the defender, not the aggressor.

   –If you cannot see a face, hold your fire.

   –Prepare yourself mentally.

   –Do not ever bluff with a weapon.

7. Coming home to a burglary

   –Get out of the house.

   –Go to a safe place and phone police.

   –Make sure police know that the house has not been checked.

5

In Your Car And
On The Road

Lock It

Locking your car is one of the easiest and most effective deterrents to crime. Unfortunately, it is often the most overlooked. Since the majority of criminals are opportunists, you give yourself a good measure of protection when you place an obstacle like a locked car door in their path. The doors should also be locked when you are driving. People have been surprised at traffic signals by a criminal opening the door and grabbing a purse or pulling the driver from the car and stealing it. Keep your doors locked and also keep the windows rolled up in dangerous areas.

When running a quick errand into a store or bank, it is easy to talk yourself into leaving the car unlocked. After all, you are only going to be away from your vehicle for "five minutes!" The problem arises when, in that same mad dash, you get in your car and drive away without noticing the person who is lying down on the floor in the back.

"Woman Raped" is the headline in the police section of today's paper. "A woman was abducted at 10:30 p.m. as she returned to her car which was parked at a shopping mall. A man armed with a ten-inch knife was hiding in the back seat and confronted the woman when she got into the car. He tied her hands and feet and made her lie down in the back seat while he drove to an unknown location where he assaulted her." You have undoubtedly read similar stories in your own local paper. It does not always happen to someone else. It could happen to you. Look into your car before you get into it.

How would you react if you found someone in your vehicle? Your plan should be to move away from the car as quickly as possible and get to safety so you can phone the police. Don't confront the intruder.

Another police officer once told me a terrifying story. A woman, we'll call her Mrs. Jones, was leaving a shopping mall one evening and found an elderly woman lying in a blanket in her back seat. She had left her car unlocked because there was "nothing in it to steal." She asked the elderly woman what she was doing in her car. The woman explained that she had been evicted from her apartment and she had been wandering around all day. She was cold and found the unlocked car and had crawled in to get warm. She then asked if she would drive her to a shelter. Mrs. Jones agreed, but said that she would first have to return to the mall to phone her husband and tell him that she would be late. Mrs. Jones believed the woman but felt a little uncomfortable about finding a stranger in her car, so instead of phoning her husband she located a mall security guard who contacted the local police. When the police arrived, she took them to the car. The woman was still in the car wrapped in the blanket. When the police asked her to step from the car she refused. When it was decided that she would have to be physically removed from the car, they pulled the blanket away to find that this was not an elderly woman, but a man with a hatchet.

What if it really had been an elderly woman in need of

assistance? There would have been no problem at all. The police would have taken her to the shelter. It took a little time for Mrs. Jones to track down the security guard and wait for the police. It was an inconvenience, but what would have happened if she had ordered the woman out of her car, or worse, if she had gotten in the car with her in an effort to be a Good Samaritan? You can be a Good Samaritan and still be safety conscious. A few extra steps can insure that you are offering a helping hand to someone who will thank you, rather than hurt you.

When approaching your car, remember to have the door key ready in your hand. If someone should approach you, you will be able to get into your car as quickly as possible. Many new cars on the market today have a feature that unlocks all the doors when the driver's door is unlocked. This is not necessarily a desirable feature. If someone is concealed along the passenger side, he will be able to get into your car when you do.

Parking Lots

Parking lots are a difficult place to assess danger zones. It is hard to determine legitimate from illegitimate users. Just about anyone could have a legitimate reason for being in a parking lot. You have to look at behavior and environmental hazards.

When choosing a parking space, be careful. Look for potential areas of concealment. Don't park along a wooded boundary, next to a dumpster, or along a windowless side of a building. Choose a place in the center of the lot close to other parked cars. Park in attended lots if possible. If you are parking during daylight but do not intend to leave until after dark, look for a lamppost and park under or near it. Do not park next to a car that is occupied by anyone who makes you uncomfortable. It might be a great parking space, but if you are not comfortable leaving the safety of your car, move to another spot.

Before you get out, take just ten seconds to look around you. What do you see? Are there any potential hazards? Is the parking lot completely void of movement? It might be better to wait a few more seconds to see if someone else parks; maybe someone will leave the building and walk toward their car while you are leaving yours. You are much better off if there is normal activity going on around you before you get out. An active area is not a desirable environment for criminals. Once you have detected normal activity, proceed with caution. Don't let your guard down. Remember to keep the brain and body functioning together. Concentrate on the area that lies between you and your destination. Remember your plan.

This happened to me. I was leaving a department store last year in the middle of the afternoon and noticed that there was no activity in the parking lot. I waited at the front of the store for a few minutes to see if anyone else was coming out. No one did. I was struggling with my packages and late for a lunch date so I looked around quickly and headed for my car. When I was halfway across the lot I saw a young man walking in my direction. I couldn't figure out where he had come from, as I had not seen him earlier. I picked up my pace a little, and so did he. "Miss," he began to yell, now approaching much faster, "I'm conducting a survey for college. I'd just like to ask you a few questions."

I reached my car, set my packages on the ground, unlocked my door—my key, of course, was already in my hand. I got in and locked the door as I closed it. "Come on, lady, I'm not a rapist. I just wanted to ask you a few questions for this survey!" he said. I rolled my window down a few inches and said, "I don't know who you are. Now get away from my car!" I looked at his hands. He had his pen poised as though he were going to write down answers for his survey, but he wasn't holding paper, he was holding a wallet. It was obvious that he wasn't taking a survey. Now my stomach started to tighten. "I said to get away from my car. Now." I ordered and this time he did. Had he not, I would have simply driven away and left my packages on the ground. After he had gone to the other side of the lot, I collected my packages and drove to a pay phone at the service station across the street, where I called the police. I watched the young man walk out of the parking lot before the police could arrive. They could not have done anything since no crime had been committed, but I would like to have had him identified, he was definitely up to no good.

Hitchhiking

The simple rule here is never to hitchhike and never pick up hitchhikers. A criminal is usually looking for someone who is vulnerable or careless. Picking up a hitchhiker or hitching a ride will make you appear extremely vulnerable and extremely careless. You may feel sorry for the person seeking a ride. He or she may look needy and harmless, but looks can deceive. If the person looks as though he needs assistance, stop at a safe location and call the police. Let them take care of it.

Breakdowns

Your plan for car breakdowns should begin with preventive maintenance. Don't just fill the car with gas and drive it until it leaves you stranded somewhere. Follow these very simple rules:

1. Check your tire pressure weekly.

2. Have a spare tire in the car and know how to change it.

3. If you are having car trouble and are not able to fix it, avoid traveling alone or late at night.

4. Never let your gas gauge drop below a quarter of a tank.

5. Keep a white cloth under the front seat. A white flag hanging outside your window when you are stopped, signals that you are disabled and need assistance. If you do not have a white cloth, raise the hood.

6. If you have the means, a car phone is an ideal safety precaution.

7. Keep a set of battery cables in your trunk and know how to use them.

If a breakdown should occur, first check your surroundings. If it's the middle of the afternoon and you've had the good fortune to break down in front of a busy shopping center or in your own neighborhood, you are likely to feel comfortable getting out and finding a pay phone. The difficult decisions come when it is late at night or you are stranded on a deserted roadway. Even a major interstate could be a dangerous place to leave the safety of your car. Criminals travel that interstate just like the rest of us. The other drivers speeding by will barely notice you, let alone watch you long enough to see that you are about to be abducted by the Good Samaritan who stopped to "assist" you.

If you find yourself broken down on the side of the road where it is not safe for you to locate immediate assistance, you should:

1. Stay in your car. It may seem only a short walk to the exit ramp, but being on foot makes you entirely too vulnerable to would-be rapists or robbers.

2. Drape a white cloth from your car window to indicate that you need help. Turn your emergency flashers on. If you have a "Call Police" banner, set it up in your rear window. If you need to get out of your car long enough to set out an emergency flare or raise your hood, do so, especially if it is dark and your car is difficult to see.

3. When someone finally stops to assist you, keep your doors locked and your windows up except for an inch or so.

4. Ask the person to go to the next exit and make a phone call for you. Ask them to call the police, your spouse, a

specified tow truck or whoever you need to assist you. If the person says he or she has some mechanical aptitude and may be able to correct the problem, pop the hood release, but do not get out of your car.

5. Do not accept a ride to a service station. It could turn out to be a much longer ride than you had in mind.

6. If a tow truck arrives and you did not summon it, think twice before accepting assistance. If you did not send for the truck, there may be no record of it stopping to assist you. Before you accept help, ask the driver to summon the police on his radio.

Exercising patience will be the most difficult part of this plan. It will aggravate you to sit and wait when you know you are perfectly capable of making that one-or two-mile walk to the service station. Unfortunately there is more to consider than the physical challenge.

You could "what if" this plan until the cows come home. What if it's 10 degrees outside? What if you have two toddlers in the car who need food and a change of diapers? What if you are offered a ride by a priest driving a church bus loaded with nuns?

You will be the only one who has enough information to decide whether to accept some offers of assistance. It will take discipline and patience to make the safest choice for you. The safest choice is rarely the most convenient.Weigh your options carefully. In most cases, time will be on your side.

When is a Police Officer not a Police Officer?
You are alone, it's late at night, and you are driving on a nearly deserted road. Suddenly you see blue flashing lights in your rearview mirror and you know you have to pull over.

Police impersonators do not turn up very often, but they are out there and they can be dangerous. How will you know the difference between a police impersonator who intends to do you harm and the real McCoy who may write you a ticket or arrest you if you do not pull over?

First, do not forget about the possibility that it might not be a real police officer. Impersonators rely on the fact that their victims will be flustered and anxious to comply with their requests. When you notice the flashing lights and siren behind you, you know you are required to yield to that vehicle. It may be that the emergency vehicle is simply trying to pass you. Merge slowly to the right and see if it is passing or staying with you. Once it is clear that this is an intended traffic stop, see if there is a nearby convenience store, shopping center, or other populated or well-lighted area and wait until you reach that location before stopping your vehicle. Make sure you are not speeding to reach this location. You don't want to give the impression you are trying to get away. If there is not a safe location in the immediate area, pull over to the right and stop.

Notice the emergency equipment on the car, if you can. A "marked" police car has a light bar on the roof; an unmarked police car has lights in the grill or on the dashboard. If it is a marked police car, most of your worries are over. It is very hard to falsely obtain a marked police cruiser. When a uniformed officer emerges from a marked cruiser you can stop worrying about whether or not it is a real police officer and start worrying about whether or not your tags are current!

If it is an unmarked car, tune in your instincts. Anyone can buy a set of grill lights or a dashboard bubble light. Don't start rummaging to find your license and registration, there will be plenty of time for that. Keep your hands on the steering wheel, your door locked, and your window rolled up most of the way. Watch your rear view mirror to see what steps out of the unmarked car. If it is a uniformed officer, you can relax a bit. When the officer approaches the car, look for the indications that it is a police uniform and not a "security guard" uniform. Look for the state or city seal or the patch or badge that has the word "police" across it. Look for the side-arm (gun) and for the police radio located on the officer's belt, or clipped to the uniform shirt around the pocket. These are all indications that the person standing next to your door is a police officer. The glare from the officer's spotlight may blind you until the officer is at your door. This is a safety precaution used by police and should not alarm you. The presence of more than one police vehicle is also a very good indication that there is no danger of foul play.

If the person who steps from the emergency vehicle is not in uniform, be a little more leery. There is still a good chance that this is a police officer and not an impersonator. It may be a plainclothes detective, a federal officer, or an officer on a plainclothes assignment. Treat this person as an officer, but be careful. Unless it is an emergency, in which case there will probably be more than one officer, the officer will begin by presenting a badge and an identification card. Do not settle for a quick flash. Ask the officer to hold it up to the window so you can look at it. Check it for the word "police" or "federal agent" and match the picture to the person standing before you. The name or seal on the badge should match the agency he claims to represent.

If he is a police officer he will probably ask for your identification. Police impersonators often walk up, flash a badge, and try to open the door. This all happens very fast so that they can keep you off guard. If you are asked to unlock the door and get out, and you have reason to suspect this is not a police officer, stay in your car and ask the officer to use his police radio to call for an additional officer. A police officer will have this capability, an impersonator will not. Explain why you're apprehensive. Do not become argumentative or defensive. Cooperate with this person as much as you can without leaving the safety of your car. Simply say why you're scared and ask for another officer to be summoned.

Some police agencies have a policy of ordering the driver from the vehicle by using their loudspeaker. This practice keeps the officer from having to approach the car and brings the person out into the open. You may want to contact your local law enforcement agency sometime just to determine what is to be expected in the event of a traffic stop by one of their officers.

It's essential to be reasonable in your suspicion. Police officers have a job to do and your being stopped at night is not reason enough to suspect foul play. Don't assume that because you have not committed an offense this must be an impersonator. You might have a burned-out taillight, expired plates, or appear to be drunk because you were trying to tune a radio station and weaved momentarily.

In more rural parts of the country, requesting an additional officer may be difficult to do. There might only be one officer for many square miles. You had better be able to justify why you are refusing to get out if ordered to do so. If you have just cause and your instincts are warning you of danger, sit tight and keep your hands on the steering wheel. If you meet with refusal to produce another officer, or the situation takes a turn that makes it clear you are not dealing with a police officer, obey the speed limit and drive to the nearest police station or public area to obtain assistance.

Traffic Accidents

Odds are you will be involved in at least one traffic accident in your lifetime. When you are involved in a collision, you must stop, summon help for anyone injured, and identify yourself for insurance purposes. For your own safety, try to be aware of the surroundings even though you may be stunned or hurt.

Criminals may cause or take advantage of a minor accident just to get you stopped and out of your car. Be very careful when this happens in a danger zone. For example: It is the middle of the night and you are alone at a red light. The car behind you rolls into your car, tapping your bumper and breaking a taillight. The other driver, whether he or she intends foul play or not, will get out of his or her car to assess the damage. Remain locked inside your car and roll your window down a little. If you determine that the other driver

41

intends no harm, suggest moving out of the roadway to an open service station or convenience store to exchange information. Fender benders are not often used as a ploy, but it has happened and you should be aware of it.

Fender benders, unlike major accidents, are most likely to occur at low speeds in congested areas, so the likelihood of having an attentive audience of other drivers is pretty good. Be sure to jot down the license of the other car in case the driver decides not to follow you to the service station. Many people remain in the middle of the road because they believe the police will not investigate an accident once the cars have been moved. This is untrue. Officers would much rather have you move your car out of the flow of traffic, making it safer for you and for other drivers. Witness and driver statements, damage, and skid marks will all work together to allow the officer to recreate the accident. If there are no injuries, the first thing an officer will have you do is clear the vehicles from the roadway anyway. Don't jeopardize your safety by remaining stopped in the middle of traffic.

Try to control yourself when someone is discourteous or abusive to you. Don't give other drivers a dirty look or insulting gesture, don't drive up next to them to shout. Learn to let these things roll off. Don't cut someone off because they cut you off or drive with your high beams on the car in front because it won't let you pass. If someone does this to you, ignore it. If you let your emotions get the best of you, you may find yourself face to face with someone who carries a gun. These incidents have a tendency to escalate rapidly and get out of hand.

If You Are Followed

If you suspect you are being followed by someone, do not go home. While it is a normal reaction for you to want to get to a place where you feel safe, you don't want this person to know where you live. There are no clear signs that will indicate that you are being followed. Your instincts will probably be the driving force here. If you suspect you are being followed, make a few turns down active streets and see if the car follows you. If it does and you feel that you are being followed, drive to the nearest police station, fire station, or open store and call the police. They will not be able to make an arrest for following you, but they will be able to identify or deter the person.

Don't talk yourself out of being cautious. Some criminals follow women home and watch the house. They break in in the middle of the night after they determine that there are no other adults in the house. If you think you are being followed, do not go home. If you are parked and a vehicle blocks your path, making it impossible for you to drive away, stay in the car with the doors locked. Do not argue with the person, for you may make matters worse. Sound the horn continuously until they leave or help arrives.

If someone tries to run you off the road and there is no indication that it is an emergency vehicle, try not to panic. Blow your horn to attract attention and try to keep moving. Do not pull off into a driveway or down a side street. If you are forced over to the side of the road, keep your doors locked and keep sounding the horn to draw attention. Once they have stopped their car and gotten out, start driving or backing away from them, then drive to safety.

Public Transportation

When using public transportation, you should plan your route in advance. Don't stand at the bus stop any longer than necessary. If you are early for your bus, go into a nearby store until it is time for your bus to arrive. Always keep your children in sight while on the bus. Don't put your belongings on the seat beside you or on the bench at the bus stop. Don't announce your travel plans with strangers making polite conversation. It is also best not to sit near an exit door. These people are often the targets of robbers who grab purses and run when the doors open.

When you are using a cab for transportation, you should try to avoid using "bootleg" cabs. These are cabs that do not belong to companies. They are individuals driving their personal vehicles and offering cab service. They are usually a little cheaper, but they are not safer.

When using the services of a licensed taxi cab, make a mental note of the drivers name, which should be in plain view on the passenger's visor, and say it. "Mr. Green, I need to go to First and Broadway." If you become uncomfortable, get out of the cab. It is best to wait until you are in a populated area. Do not worry about personal belongings. If you believe you're in danger, get out. After getting out of the cab, you should go to a phone and call the cab company. Depending on the circumstances, you may decide to phone the police as well. Report the incident to the cab company and determine if they expect payment for the cab ride to that point. Otherwise, you might end up being criminally charged for failing to pay for the services of the cab.

Review

–Keep doors locked and windows rolled up.

–Wait until there is "normal activity" before leaving or going to your car.

–Have your door key in hand.

–Identify hazards and react: Avoid, escape, retreat.

–Don't hitchhike or pick up hitchhikers.

–Take preventive steps to avoid or prepare for a breakdown.

–Don't get out of the car or accept a ride if you break down.

–When dealing with a plainclothes officer in an unmarked car, keep doors locked and check badge and ID card carefully.

–If being followed, don't go home.

–Don't become involved in arguments with other drivers in traffic.

–If you can't drive away and are being detained by someone who may cause you harm, lock the doors and sound the horn.

–Don't stand at bus stops any longer than necessary.

–Don't sit next to the doors on a bus.

–Don't use "bootleg" cabs.

–Note the cab driver's name and say it aloud.

6

OUT AND ABOUT

Most of us are not as comfortable out in public as we are in our own homes. This may make us more alert, but it could also make us appear more vulnerable to criminals.

Sexual Harassment at Work

It is important to recognize sexual harassment in the workplace as a danger zone. It is a form of misconduct and sexual discrimination which undermines the employment relationship. Sexual harassment can be a warning sign preceding acquaintance rape—being raped by someone you know. What might be viewed as friendly behavior or harmless flirting to one person might be viewed as harassment by another. That is why it is very important to make your feelings known when someone has made you uncomfortable.

You may be reluctant to take action because you want to be well liked at work and you do not want to be viewed as a troublemaker. Other women in the office may not appear to be offended by the same actions that make you uncomfortable, but you must be true to yourself. If you are uncomfortable, you must take some action. In a work environment, the problem is not likely to disappear. If someone is making you uncomfortable with unwanted remarks or physical contact, put that person on notice.

State that you are not comfortable with the way you are being treated and that you intend to inform a supervisor if the behavior does not stop immediately. Tell trusted coworkers about the situation in the event that the problem should continue or escalate. You may need their support when this person is around or when the situation has to be brought to the attention of a supervisor. Do not permit the misconduct to continue without addressing it in some manner. Do not apologize to this person for being uncomfortable. Be firm and professional. If the behavior continues, follow through by making a formal complaint. Regardless of any action taken by the supervisor, the message will be loud and clear: Back off!

Intruders in the Work Place

Intruders can gain access to a work site in many ways. False documentation may be used to get by security guards. Intruders might enter through a back or side door left unlocked or standing open. They might walk in with other employees. Their motivations range from theft of purses and calculators to corporate espionage, rape, and assault. Intruders often pose as delivery people, repair workers, phone repair workers, or movers. Just because someone has on a tool belt does not mean he belongs there. Employees are not likely to challenge the presence of a stranger unless strict guidelines are mandated by management.

Security specialists recommend that employees wear picture ID's and all visitors wear a special visitor's badge. Thus, anyone not wearing a badge will stand out. There should also be a policy which dictates how employees should report a stranger in the work place. The policy should indicate who should be called to verify whether or not the stranger belongs there and what action should be taken if it is determined that this person is unauthorized.

Employees who work alone in an office are at much higher risk. If you periodically work late when others have gone home, you are putting yourself in a danger zone. Bathrooms, elevators, stairwells, and parking lots should also be considered potentially hazardous areas. The following preventive measures are recommended:

1. Keep the office door locked when working late or coming in early. These are the high risk hours. If you are approached while working in an office alone, imply that someone else is in the office or is expected soon. If it is a person you do not know, you might try yelling down the hall or to a back office, "Bill, Mr. Jones is here!" Then say to the stranger, "I'm so glad to finally meet you. Bill must be getting coffee, but he'll be with us in a minute. Would you like some before we get started?" If it is a person you know, but are not comfortable with, you might say, "Oh, I thought you were Bill Stevens. He was supposed to be here five minutes ago, and we have a lot to cover today." This would indicate that someone will be there soon. In the meantime you can leave the office under the pretense of going for coffee or to the copier.

2. Do not get on an elevator with a person who looks suspicious to you or makes you feel uncomfortable. If the doors open and you don't want to get in, step back and say, "Go ahead."

3. If you are already on the elevator and begin to feel uncomfortable, push the button for the closest floor and exit. If you are followed, go to an occupied office.

4. When walking to your car after work, pair up with another employee and walk out together. Or ask available security guards or doormen to escort you. If appropriate, tip them.

5. Avoid using stairwells when you are alone.

6. If your restroom facilities are also open to the public, ask a coworker to accompany you. At the very least let someone know where you are going and that you expect to be back momentarily. Even employee-only restrooms should be visually scanned before entering alone.

Shopping

Whenever possible, shop in an area that you are familiar with. Remember that shopping with a companion is safer than shopping alone. When you are writing out checks, be sure that no one is looking over your shoulder. If the clerk asks for a phone number, take the check back and write it down rather than saying it out loud.

Do not give out too much information when engaged in casual conversation with store personnel. My friend Pattie was standing in line behind a woman who was chatting with the cashier as she wrote out her check. The woman was explaining that her husband was overseas for several weeks and she and her infant son were very lonely as they had no family in the area. Her address and phone number on her check were in plain view for other people in line to see.

Store and mall restrooms are seldom located in areas that you will feel comfortable in. They are usually at the back of the store near delivery bays and rear exits or at the end of long isolated hallways. Consider stopping at a safe place to use the restroom before you get to the store. Or, plan to patronize only stores with amenable facilities when you intend to be there for an extended period of time.

Airports

Criminals who work airports are usually cunning and experienced. Stay alert. Don't allow people to move in too closely to you. Be wary of the space around your body. Follow airline regulations and check as many items as you can. Don't load yourself down while waiting for your flight. Use only your initials and last name on your luggage tag. Put a work address and phone number on the tag, rather than your home address. Should a burglar get a look at the address tag, he or she will know that you are going to be away and will now have your address.

Before hailing a cab from the airport, obtain information about your destination. Contact the hotel or the people you will be staying with and find out how far it is from the airport to your destination and what is the most direct route. With this information you will be able to say to the cab driver, "Mr. Green, I need to go to Motel 1 on Union Street. It's about eight miles down Interstate 95." This will make you appear much less vulnerable and will reduce your chances of being cheated or abducted.

Hotels and Motels

You may be in the habit of always using one particular chain of hotels. If you are traveling to an area that you are unfamiliar with, you may want to call the local police department to double check your selection. Tell the desk officer or duty sergeant that you are planning to stay at Motel 1 and ask if it is located in an area that the police would consider safe. If the officer advises that it is not the best area in town, ask for a recommendation. This is not fail-safe, but the police know which areas are considered safe and which are not. If the officer prefers not to answer for the police department, ask if he would have his own family stay there.

Do not leave valuables in plain view in your vehicle in the hotel parking lot. All valuables should be taken inside or locked in the trunk.

Always have a bellhop escort you to your room. Ask him to check it out before you enter. Look around every time you go to your room. Once inside, you should check to see that all locks are functioning. If the locks are malfunctioning, ask for another room. Try to avoid ground floor rooms whenever possible. Like ground floor apartments, these are more accessible to nighttime burglars and rapists. Check that your phone is working and that the numbers to the hotel desk, security, and the police are listed. Stay alert when using ice and snack machines. These areas are usually isolated and can be hazardous. Do not leave your room door ajar while you go to the ice machine. Keep doors and windows locked, regardless of what floor you are on. Use the peephole to identify visitors. Verify hotel staff by calling the front desk before opening the door to anyone.

Outdoor Exercising

A good exercise routine is healthy for mind and body. You should incorporate your safety practices into your exercise routine. Some special considerations include:

1. Exercise with a partner. This will increase your safety a great deal. Remember, the safest way is not always the most practical.

2. A dog can be an excellent deterrent to violent crime if the weather and the physical stamina of your pet allow it.

3. Clothes that are too loose are also easy to grab, making you a desirable target.

4. If you wear glasses, always wear them jogging or biking. You have to be able to see a hazard before you can avoid it.

5. Stay next to main roads and populated areas. Do not use wooded jogging paths or isolated paths next to rivers.Wooded areas provide lots of hiding places. Be familiar with the routes you plan to take. If you exercise alone, someone should know the route you plan to take and when you expect to return. Vary your route and exercise time occasionally to avoid being too predictable.

6. If you use a handheld stereo with headset, you are disabling one of the senses that might alert you to danger. You are also tuning out your mind from the present moment. And, you look vulnerable.

7. If you live in an area that you know is dangerous, don't exercise alone there. Take up an indoor sport, join a club with an indoor track, or only exercise outdoors when you can arrange to have a partner.

Yes, you should be able to exercise any time you want, anywhere you want. But the victims of the past have taught us that the price for that type of freedom can be very, very high. You have options. Exercise them.

Recreation Areas

When using recreation areas such as parks, beaches, or open fields, leave the extras at home. Don't bring your purse, your five-hundred-dollar camera, and every credit card you own. Lock unnecessary belongings in the trunk of your vehicle or leave it at home. In parks, use well-traveled paths; know where the ranger station is in case you need assistance. At beaches, stay near lifeguard stands. Do not use public restrooms alone. Recreation areas should be avoided at night. Areas that are safe and crowded with people during the day can become extremely hazardous at night. A midnight stroll along the seashore might sound very invigorating, but after dark, beaches are magnets for criminal activity. The chances of a criminal finding a victim alone and isolated are excellent. Even couples in these areas could find themselves in danger after hours. Use recreation facilities as they were intended to be used. Any other use can jeopardize your personal safety.

Review

At work:

1. Do not allow sexual harassment at work to go unaddressed.

2. Verify repair workers in your office, especially if you are alone.

3. Keep office or shop doors locked before and after hours.

Shopping:

1. Shop with a companion when possible.

2. Do not verbally give out personal information, such as address and phone, when there are other patrons around.

3. Be very cautious when using public restrooms.

Airports and Hotels:

1. Check as much of your luggage as you can.

2. Be aware of other people near you.

3. Know in advance what your final destination is and what the most direct route is.

4. Check out your hotel with local authorities before choosing it.

5. Have a bellhop accompany you to your room and check it before you enter.

6. Check all locks once you are inside your room.

Outdoor Exercising:

1. Avoid isolated areas.

2. Exercise with a partner.

3. Stay alert.

Recreation Areas:

1. Do not use after hours.

2. Know where the ranger or lifeguard station is.

3. Use the facility as it was designed to be used.

7

Self-Defense Options

Up until this point, prevention has been the issue. Opportunity is a big part of a successful crime. When opportunity is hindered, the crime is less likely to occur. But we know that opportunity is not the only factor. There are many variables that we as individuals cannot control.

If you become the victim of violent crime, such as rape, robbery, or assault, you will have a split second to decide how to respond and maximize your survival. In order to formulate your plan ahead of time, you will need to know all of the options that you have.

The Escalation of Violence

In order to identify your options you have to look at self-defense on a scale. If you begin at the bottom—low degree of violence—you leave other options open. If you begin somewhere in the middle, you eliminate many of your options. If you begin at the top—high degree of violence—you only have one option: fight for your life and pray that you will win. Needless to say, starting at the lower end of the scale will increase your chances for survival. Escape, of course, is always your best move when confronted with violent crime, but if you are unable to escape you may have to use some form of self-defense to survive. Study your options and make as many choices as you can today, so that you will be more prepared tomorrow.

Escape

If you see the attacker approaching and have an escape route, take it. Get into your car, back on the elevator, or run back to the store. Maybe there is someone close by you can run to or signal for help. Avoiding actual confrontation is the best way to go whenever possible. You will have to react quickly. If you cannot escape, here are some other options.

Passive

In a sexual assault attack, passive response options would include:

1. Passing out. Some women fake a fainting spell, some actually faint. Where the attack takes place has a lot to do with whether or not this will be a successful tactic. If you are on an isolated jogging path or parked along a woodline, it is highly probable that you will be dragged away and attacked. If you are in a parking lot full of cars and have to be physically picked up and carried away, the sexual assault is less likely to occur.

   If you are faking it, be convincing. Drop like a sack of flour. Try to let the keys fall under the car on the way down. While the attacker is fishing for the keys, you may have an opportunity to get up and make a run for it. One drawback of this tactic is that you are likely to receive a kick in face or ribs before the attacker flees the area.

2. D-ter. D-ter is a chemical. It is a small vial about the size of an ammonia capsule and it is activated in much the same way. The victim has it handy—in a coat pocket, for example—then breaks it in the event of an attack. There

are no words to describe how awful D-ter smells. It is the ultimate in stink bombs! The company that markets it says that the smell is so bad that it is likely to make the victim and the attacker physically ill. The idea is that if you are standing there, stinking to high heaven and vomiting, a successful sexual attack is unlikely to occur.

D-ter is something that you do to yourself, not something that you have to do to the attacker. This is a good option for those who feel the other tactics discussed here would be impossible for them to do. D-ter sells for $9.95 and includes a neutralizer capsule. If you are interested, contact the company: 3D Marketing, P.O. Box 2093, Edison, NJ 08818 (908-225-0004).

3. Bodily voiding. Urination, defecation, and vomiting are also passive options. The idea is to make yourself repulsive enough that the attacker will not be able to continue. This will be more effective on some attackers than on others. Keep your back-up plan in mind.

Passive/Aggressive
This is the next step on the scale, the "brains over brawn" theory of self-defense. Use your imagination and wit to keep yourself safe until an opportunity to escape presents itself. This option may not be feasible if the attacker is severely impaired by alcohol or drugs. If your words are being comprehended, even if they are not working as quickly as you had hoped, do not abandon the approach. If the attacker is listening at all, you have a chance for this option to be effective.

1. Cooperation. Tell the attacker that you intend to cooperate fully. Convince him that there is no need to tie you up or harm you. For instance, say that you have kids at home and you are not going to do anything that is going to get you hurt; say that you would rather be raped than

die; say that you will do exactly as he says. This is not begging or pleading; these are statements of fact. The idea is to convince the criminal that you have resigned yourself to the attack. You want him to let down his guard long enough for you to escape when an opportunity presents itself. It may mean that you submit to a rape. If he has a weapon, or if you are accosted in your home or in an empty office building, or if you do not feel that you are capable of any other options, cooperation may be your only hope of survival. The decision is one that only you can make for yourself.

2. Stalling for time. This true story is, to me, an excellent example of brains over brawn.

Judy worked at a mall and was about to get in her car to leave for the day. It was a little after 5 p.m. and the parking lot was full of cars, so she felt safe. As she put the key in the door, a man came up behind her and grabbed her wrist. The man said "Let's just get in the car."

Without missing a beat, Judy wheeled around and said, "Well, you must be Mike! Janice said you were going to meet me inside! I've never been on a blind date before! I was going to wait inside but I thought you must have changed your mind. Do you want to eat here or somewhere else? We can take my car unless you want to drive." On and on and on she talked. She didn't let the attacker get a word in edgewise! She talked on and on, gesturing with her hands and completely befuddling the attacker's plan. He let go of her wrist and was trying to tell her what was going on. As she talked, she moved a few inches from him with every sentence.

When she saw a nearby couple walking through the parking lot, she said, "I don't believe this. There's John and Olivia Campbell. Yoo hoo! John! Let me say a quick hello;

I'll be right back." She quickly walked toward the couple and asked them to walk her back inside.

The attacker was beaten at this point. She had foiled his plan. He had no backup plan for being mistaken as a date! If it had gone on long enough, he might have tried to put a stop to her rambling, but Judy bought herself just enough time to locate an escape.

Another way of buying time is to divert the attention of the attacker. Ask him to stop for a pack of cigarettes or a six pack of beer "to calm your nerves." You can always ask and see if he agrees to do it. If your attacker stops, an opportunity to escape or at least signal for help may present itself.

How to stall is limited only by your imagination. In using your wit, you have an endless array of plans you can create. You might try convincing the person that you have AIDS. "If you are going to do this, I am not going to stop you. But I am HIV positive and if you get AIDS I am not going to be held liable. My attorney says that all I have to do is make it known."

You may not want to make up a story, so use what you have. A woman whose entire life revolved around the church, used what she had. When attacked, she fell down on her knees and started begging the Lord to forgive this man for what he was about to do to her. It worked! The guy walked away shaking his head saying, "Oh no, not one of those."

Another woman responded to her attack by swinging her arms and fists in complete terror and panic. Her attacker outweighed her by 150 pounds and had completely covered her mouth and nose with his hand. Realizing that she was getting nowhere, she stopped fighting and got control of herself. She knew that without oxygen, she would soon be defenseless. She could not remove his hand so she worked on the one finger that was covering her nose. She would pry it off, take a breath then let it go. As he was dragging her past a house where the lights were on, she could see people inside.

As they got closer, she realized that the windows were open. When they were directly in front of the house, she ripped his hand away and yelled for help. The occupants came out and the would-be rapist ran off.

She showed admirable presence of mind. Your own survival instincts will direct you as long as you stay in the fight. If you panic and your brain turns off, you leave your body there to fend for itself. Have a plan. Live it in your mind. Make sure it is realistic for you. Then if the worst happens, execute it.

Active Resistance

Screaming is a good example of active resistance. Whistles, air horns, and other noise-making devices designed to draw attention to the attacker also work. You are sending a clear message to the attacker that it is your intention not to cooperate.

Many experts believe that active resistance in the first seconds of an attack give the victim an excellent chance of escape. But at the same time, you probably increase your chances of becoming seriously injured or killed. Other experts believe that the odds for escape do not outweigh the probability that you will be injured and so you should remain passive. There is no definitive answer. It depends on your environment and your personal limitations. There is no point screaming or sounding a whistle if no one is likely to hear it. On the other hand, if there is a good chance that someone will hear it, you will probably thwart the attack. By staying alert and constantly scanning your environment prior to the attack, you will already know what your chances are of successfully alerting someone.

Some victims have reported that they wanted to scream but were physically unable to. You may begin with a passive approach and then scream once you find yourself in close proximity to other people. If you do scream, make it effective. Give it everything you've got! Don't just scream. "Ahhhhhh" could mean anything. Scream words—scream what is happening. "Help me! I don't know this man!" "Someone call the police! I'm being attacked." Onlookers who see a man and woman engaged in a physical altercation are more likely to assume it is a domestic dispute than rape. People will rarely step between a man and woman involved in a personal quarrel. So make sure that onlookers won't misunderstand. If you decide to scream, get all the mileage out of it that you can. If your scream's unsuccessful, you may be in danger of severe assault or being tied up. Both of these repercussions will cripple your chances of escape.

Fighting. If you decide to fight, be swift and effective. Self-defense courses can be beneficial as long as they are not taken out of context. These courses teach balance and confidence, how to concentrate your effort when throwing a punch, and how to fall without breaking bones. All of these techniques are good and are likely to serve you well in the event of an attack. But a six-week karate course at the YMCA will not make you into a self-defense expert. Unless you are in the habit of shoulder throwing your spouse to the carpet at the end of every day, it is unlikely that you will retain the moves necessary to incapacitate an attacker.

Attackers don't play fair. They will not "set up" for you. Attacks happen so fast and without warning, so it is highly unlikely that you will be able to successfully execute a self-defense move from the onset. It is more likely that you will decide to fight because every other option has failed. It will be a matter of deciding that you are willing to risk personal injury or death to attempt an escape.

Once you have decided to fight there is no turning back. There are many vulnerable areas of the body, but your best success will come by targeting the groin or the eyes. Physical strength is not necessary to incapacitate an attacker in these areas. Timing and a direct hit, however, are crucial. If the attacker figures out what you are trying to do, or you are unsuccessful in your first attempt, you are likely to pay for it. This is why a full commitment is necessary.

1. Oppose the thumb. When trying to release yourself

from the attacker's grasp, be deliberate in your moves. Don't just push and pull and exhaust yourself. Oppose the thumb. The attacker's hand cannot maintain a hold if his thumb is disengaged. Oppose the thumb and pull it away or bend it back from the hand. This will only be a temporary setback and the attacker is likely to recover quickly. A follow up measure, preferably escape, will have to be swift.

2. Kick. The legs are one of your most powerful assets but accuracy can be a problem. Save your leg strength for running. A kick or a knee in the groin will only be affective if it is a direct hit and if his clothing does not impede the strike. A better option is to wait until the genitals are exposed and then crush and twist the testicles in your hand. This is likely to put the attacker into shock and could even kill him. Pretend to cooperate until this point in the attack.

3. Gouge the eyes. Rather than trying to stick your keys in the eyes of the attacker, gouge the eyes with your thumbs. Try to dislodge them from their sockets. The eye is only held by one optic nerve, so a direct hit can do it.

These are high-risk moves and should only be used in cases where all other options have been exhausted and you have decided that submission is not a personal option or you are convinced that the attacker intends to kill you. This might be an instinctive conclusion or an obvious one. If you decide to seek physical defense tactics training, keep your other options in mind as well.

Weapons. This is the top of the scale. You not only want to escape the attacker's grasp, but intend to do him bodily harm. The most dangerous aspect is that your goal will be obvious to your attacker; and thus there is a possibility that the attacker will take your weapon and use it on you. In many cases bodily force is the only weapon an attacker may have until he is able to get control of the victim's weapon. And quite often that is just what happens.

1. Mace—Make sure that the canister of Mace or pepper spray has not expired. If you intend to use it as a weapon, it should be in your hand, not your purse, when you enter danger zones. Do not use it as an excuse to ignore personal safety practices. Mace is by no means fail-safe. In fact, a reported reaction to Mace is anger, not deterrence. You might make matters much worse.

2. Stun Guns—Too many things could go wrong with a stun gun. If it is taken away from you or used on you while it is still in your hands, you will be left completely defenseless.

3. Knives—If you can get to it, will you be able to use it? It takes a great deal of force to effectively stab someone through clothing, as well as a strong stomach on the part of the person wielding the knife. You must be very close to your attacker to make a knife work for you.

4. Guns—It is not legal to carry a gun concealed in any way. Having it strapped to your hip in plain view is not a likely scenario, and may even be illegal in some states.

I do not recommend weapons as part of your plan, but if you decide to use one you need to be comfortable with it. You need to hold it, practice with it, and obtain training if training is available.

Keep in mind that you could go from passive to active resistance in a matter of seconds. Knowing your options can give you an edge. When constructing your plan, review all your self-defense options carefully. Identify the advantages and disadvantages of each. Most important, look inward to determine what you are honestly capable of doing if attacked.

Review

The escalation of violence
Passive: Least amount of physical demand

1. Passing out

2. Urination, defecation, or vomiting

3. D-Ter

Passive/Aggressive: Brains over brawn

1. Cooperate until escape

2. Mistaken Identity

3. Stall for time

4. Countless scenario options, be convincing

Active Resistance: Screaming

1. Includes whistles and air horns

2. Someone must hear it

3. Scream what is happening to onlookers

Fighting: High risk for serious injury

1. Swift and deliberate

2. Groin and eyes

Weapons: Not recommended

1. Can be turned on you

2. False sense of security

3. Training needed

8
RAPE

Rape is a crime of violence and hostility. Though women are most likely to be the target of rape, more and more men are reporting attacks as well. Every person is a potential victim.

It is difficult for some people to imagine rape as a violent assault rather than a sexual act. Society and the criminal justice system are quick to try and place at least some of the blame on the victim. Rape is an assault, like punching someone in the face and knocking out his teeth, only much worse. It is like someone pulling you from you car, beating you with a crow bar, and driving away with your vehicle, only much worse. It is as appalling as child molestation and as degrading as being stripped naked in a public place.

Rapists do not rape for sex, any more than an alcoholic takes a drink because he is thirsty. Rape is not about sex and no victim of rape ever wanted it to happen.

Facts About Rape

The following statistics come from a ten-year study reported in a Bureau of Justice Statistics bulletin.

1. Over a ten year period in the United States there were an estimated 1.5 million rapes.

2. 123,000 of those victims were men.

3. 55 percent of victims of rape were single (never married).

4. 66 percent of attacks occurred between 6 p.m. and 6 a.m.

5. Victims from ages 16 to 34 were most affected.

6. 36 percent of attacks occurred at or near the victim's home.

7. In 64 percent of the cases, there was no weapon used.

8. When a weapon was used, a knife was used most often.

9. 62 percent of victims did not receive compounding injuries.

Other facts:

1. Rape affects all social classes and all races.

2. Most rapists are repeat offenders.

3. An FBI study indicates that 67 percent of known rapists are married and have regular sexual relationships.

4. The FBI estimates that only 1 in 10 to 15 victims reports the crime of rape.

Statistics do not offer much help to you if you are selected as a victim, but they are necessary in order for you to understand the scope of the problem.

Why Rape Happens

Rape is committed out of a desire to control or hurt another person. It is motivated by anger and aggression.

The Power Rapist. This attacker is insecure in his own masculinity. He compensates for his feelings of inadequacy by controlling another person. This attacker often believes that women "like" to be raped and may date his victim prior to the attack. He generally does not plan to hurt his victim and is a good target for manipulation by the victim.

The Anger Rapist. This attacker is volatile and dangerous. He considers sex debasing and revolting. The rape is usually executed by this attacker as a retaliation for an imagined wrong. The attacks are often unplanned and aimed at random vulnerable victims. He usually beats and degrades his victims.

The Sadistic Rapist. The attacker uses cruelty and violence to punish the victim. The assaults are planned carefully and deliberately and often include bizarre abusive acts of terror. Surviving this attacker takes an incredible amount of will and persistence.

The Juvenile Rapist. This attacker is usually an under-achiever and a loner. The juvenile sex offender almost exclusively targets one of three groups of victims;

1. victims five years or so younger than self

2. peers

3. victims ten or more years older than self

These assaults often involve drugs, alcohol, and weapons.

Gang Rapists. These attacks are brutal and difficult to defend against. The only possible hope of escape is to try to isolate the leader from the rest of the group and convince him that your desire is to be for him only. In this situation you do not have much to lose. Even if you can convince him to move away from the others, you have a better chance at an escape.

Prevention is your best safety guideline. Review your personal safety rules often and listen to your instincts.

Acquaintance Or Date Rape

Acquaintance rape is still rape. The term "acquaintance rape" came about to make people aware that the attacker is often someone they know. The term was never intended to lessen the offense or make the victim responsible in any way. If you are raped by someone that you know, you are raped. You are entitled to as much compassion and understanding and help as any other victim of violent crime.

If someone you know steals your car, it is not your fault; it is grand theft auto. If someone you know takes money from you without your permission, it is not your fault; it is robbery. And if someone you know has sexual intercourse with you without your permission, it is not your fault; it is rape.

If this has happened to you, you may have hesitated to call it rape. Maybe you felt that because it was someone you knew, you "asked for it." It is okay to get mad about it, to feel bad about it, to want help for it. A violent crime was committed against you. That is why you feel so bad—not because you are dumb or guilty but because you are a victim. All victims of violent crime hurt in much the same way that you do. They are angry and afraid and frustrated just like you.

If the criminal justice system will not help you, then help yourself. Find someone to talk to about the attack—whether it happened yesterday or twenty years ago. Care enough about yourself to take the first step. Rape crisis centers have wonderful, caring, and professional people. Many of the volunteers have been victims themselves. They know what you are experiencing. They can help you come to terms with it and put it behind you. They will not judge or embarrass you. They can help you, but they do not know who you are. You must ask for their help.

What Causes Acquaintance Rape

These attackers generally fall into the "power rapist" category. The events that lead to this type of attack often include a mix of misread signals, misplaced expectations, and immaturity and insensitivity on the part of the attacker. Many attackers expect a certain amount of resistance and think it's part of the sexual game. But if attackers expect resistance, how will they know when resistance is real or not? They don't know. Many just act on their own desires. They rape.

Preventing Date Rape

Be aware of signs that indicate that the person is becoming too familiar. Words or actions that make you uncomfortable should be addressed on the spot.If the person shows up at your door unexpectedly when no one else is home, send him away. If he truly meant no harm, he will understand and respect your position. If an acquaintance walks you to your car or hotel room and you begin to feel uncomfortable, be very assertive and tell him to leave. Forget your manners. Make your feelings known, loud and clear. Run out of the house, lock yourself in a bathroom, call the police—or do all three. Keep verbalizing your commands for the person to leave. Do not be embarrassed. Be safe.

Date rape generally occurs early in a relationship. For this reason it is best that you go out with other couples and have a hand in planning the dates until you become more familiar and relaxed around each other.

Watch for these signs in your date:

1. *Hostility.* A hostile or insensitive view of women. Admires other women's legs or figures in your presence or makes hostile remarks about the way you or other women dress or behave.

2. *Aggression.* An extremely domineering personality. Makes all of the decisions without asking how you feel about it. Treats you as his property or talks down to you.

3. *Unrealistic expectations.* Puts you on a pedestal to the point that it is not possible for you to live up to the expectations he has for you.

Some of these characteristics may be subtle in the beginning and may be difficult to identify as a hazard. Keep things light and controlled until you feel comfortable. In the beginning of a relationship, alcohol consumption should be very moderate or avoided altogether. Pay attention to how much your date is drinking as well. Alcohol affects judgment. Keep your wits about you.

If you find yourself in an attack situation, react immediately and forcefully. State clearly what you are feeling. Forget about saving face or hurting feelings. Demand that the person back off and call for help. Flee if necessary. Then terminate the date and the relationship immediately.

In some date attacks, the attacker knows exactly what is going on. He may say that it is his word against yours. It is not likely that his intent is to harm you. If you find yourself in this situation, you may want to try to outwit him.

If you are about to be raped, do what you can. If you can't do anything, concentrate on survival. There is no shame in survival, only courage.

What To Do If You Are Raped

1. Report the crime. Taking the burden off of your shoulders and putting it onto the shoulders of the police is likely to result in an accelerated healing process. Even if the police never catch or convict the attacker, you have acknowledged the crime. You have decided to let the authorities do with it what they will. Then you can begin to concentrate on yourself.

2. Do not bathe, shower, eat or drink anything. Do not change your clothes. Your body is the crime scene. Necessary evidence of the crime must be left untouched until you can be seen by a doctor, which will be immediately. An officer may be nearby, but will not be present during the examination.

3. You can request a female officer if you prefer one. However, a male police officer is likely to be just as compassionate and have just as positive an effect on your recovery.

4. You will be put in contact with a rape crisis center either at the hospital or immediately following the attack. If you opt not to accept their services, you should seek private counseling.

A trial is likely to follow if the rapist is identified. Victim Witness Assistance Programs are set up to walk you through the criminal justice maze. Some victims are concerned that by not physically resisting, they will appear responsible for the attack. The fact is, if you have made it to court, you have won. If you are alive to talk about your attack, you have won. You can state why you responded the way you did, then let the system sort it out. You don't owe anyone an explanation for protecting yourself from harm.

Review

1. Rape is a violent assault. Do not accept blame for being a victim.

2. Rape occurs to people of all walks of life. Assuming that you will never be a victim could leave you defenseless in an attack.

3. Acquaintance rape is still rape. You are much more likely to be raped by someone that you know than by a stranger.

4. Indications to be wary for in a date acquaintance:

   Hostility toward women in general.

   Repeatedly disregards your wishes.

   An overly domineering personality that makes you uncomfortable.

   Puts you on a pedestal.

5. What to do in an acquaintance rape attack:

   Trust your instincts.

   Verbalize loud and forcefully.

   If the person will not leave, you leave.

   Cooperate briefly in order to set up an escape.

6. If you are raped:

   Report the crime. This will aid in your recovery.

   If you report it to the police, do so immediately. Do not wash, eat, or drink until after a doctor examines you.

   The police will put you in touch with a support agency. Accept help.

   Do not focus on possible outcomes of a trial. If you have survived the attack, you have won. Do not allow anyone to make you feel differently.

   If you have been a victim of rape and need help, contact a rape crisis center in your area. Do not try to heal alone.

9

TALKING TO YOUR KIDS ABOUT PERSONAL SAFETY

My law enforcement experience has given me a good understanding of what children need to know to protect themselves. You will have to decide when your child is mature enough to handle the more sensitive issues, but my guess is they will probably need the information sooner than you would like to believe. You want your child to grow up happy and carefree. You might feel like you are taking some of that away if you tell them of bad people who might want to hurt them, but it is a fact that must be dealt with. If you do not tell them how to protect themselves, you leave them defenseless.

Preschoolers
Personal Information. As soon as they are able, children should know their address, phone number, and how to pronounce and spell their last name. They should be cautioned against giving this information to anyone without their parent's permission with the exception of a doctor or nurse at a hospital or a uniformed police officer.

Authority Figures. Your child should know how to identify an authority figure in case they are ever in need of assistance. Many parents make the mistake of pointing out a police officer or police car and saying, "If you don't behave, the police officers will take you to jail." Even if you do not like the police, they are who you would want your children to come to if they were ever lost or hurt.

Take them to a local police station in your area and let them see the officers' uniforms and police cars. Make sure that they know that it is always okay to go to these uniformed persons if they need help. Point out other uniforms; remind your child of the difference between other uniforms and a police uniform. Teach them how to signal to an officer if they need assistance. They should bring their arm to their chest in a "come here" motion. If they merely wave, the officer might not realize they need assistance.

If your child is afraid of sirens, explain that police officers will not turn their sirens on if your child simply flags them down.

If the police agency in your area sponsors an open house, be sure to attend. This is an excellent way to introduce your child to police officers.

Telephone. Your child should know how to dial 9-1-1 or the appropriate emergency number in case of an emergency. Practice on a play phone; you pretend to be the emergency operator. Keep the number posted next to the phone or on an automatic dialer; caution them not to practice on a real phone.

Teach your child not to give out information on the phone about themselves or your family. If the child answers the phone, it should only be to identify the caller and nothing more. Role play this situation. Children learn faster by doing rather than listening.

Clothing. Do not buy T-shirts or jackets that have the child's name printed on the front. An abductor might seize this opportunity to call the child by name and gain his or her confidence. If you mark the child's clothing labels, mark them with your daytime phone number.

Public Restrooms. Public restrooms are dangerous for adults. They are even more hazardous for children. Do not send your child into a public restroom alone. Your little boy may be uncomfortable going into the ladies room with Mom, but that is the way it should be done until he is old enough to recognize danger.

Strangers. "Don't talk to strangers" is a broad statement and it is not easily understood. Strangers are sometimes people your child recognizes. Maintenance people, ice cream truck drivers, groundskeepers, and neighbors are "strangers," but your child is likely to know them by name. It is not safe for your child to go anywhere with any person or get into a car or go into a house without your permission. No matter what the adult offers as a reason to go. Adults they do not recognize at all should be avoided completely.

Teach your child how to protect his own body space. If a car pulls up or a person approaches them on foot, your child should know how to back away and not let the person get close enough to touch. Role playing is essential for making your child's plan work. Make it fun. Dress up in funny clothes and pretend you are driving down the street and try to talk to your child. Teach your child a plan, then practice it. Some families set up code words in case the child ever has to be picked up by a stranger in an emergency. For instance, if the parents are injured in a car accident and a stranger comes to pick them up and take them to a relative's house or the hospital, the code word might be "fish face." If the stranger identifies that code word, it is okay to go with them. However, it is very, very unlikely that a stranger rather than a known friend, a relative, or a police officer would have to pick the child up.

McGruff House. The McGruff House Program is a nationally recognized system of identifying safe homes when children are in need of assistance. Children are usually taught in elementary school to recognize the McGruff House symbol as a safe house to go to when help is needed. This program is sponsored by the National Crime Prevention Council and is usually administered by local law enforcement agencies. Applicants for this program submit an application which includes a criminal history check and receive training in how to deal with a child seeking assistance.

Molestation. Teach your children about good touching and bad touching. A good rule for your child is to never agree to keep a secret from Mommy and Daddy, no matter what anyone tells them. Don't confuse them by asking them to keep a secret, regardless of how minor, from your spouse.

Don't call a surprise a secret. Surprises, such as birthday presents, should be clearly defined and the difference is usually understood even by preschoolers. "Secret" should be a buzzword for "Tell Mommy and Daddy immediately."

Preteens

Drugs. Drug education in the schools is a good start, but it must be reinforced on the home front. If you do not have the vocabulary or the knowledge to instruct your children, there are plenty of resources. Start with your local police department's juvenile division. "Just Say No" is a great slogan, but your children will require much more instruction than that if they are going to stay out of the hands of drug dealers.

If you are using drugs yourself, you are already causing a problem.

Sex. Sexual curiosity and activity begin much sooner than parents like to think. AIDS and pregnancy are often the biggest concerns for parents, but we need to add rape to this list. No mother has ever envisioned her son as a rapist, nor has mother envisioned her son as a victim of rape—boys are just as vulnerable as girls—sometimes more so, but if the guidelines for consensual sex are not established by parents, then they are learned on the street by peers, who have also had no guidance.

A six-year-old boy came home from school one day and announced that he was in the "least sexually advanced" group. He explained the least sexually advanced group sat on the swings with the girls, the medium sexual advanced group kissed the girls, and the most sexual advanced group pushed the girls down on the ground and laid on top of them! There is a street education network that you know nothing about. Your child is going to be exposed to it no matter what precautions you take. Do not send them out in the world to fend for themselves.

Adolescent boys need to know that an affirmative "yes" must be obtained first. Not an assumed yes. Not a "she-didn't-stop-me yes." The word yes.

Girls and boys need to know there is no shame in making a scene if someone is doing something that they do not like. Even if it starts out feeling "okay," as in kissing and petting. When it stops feeling okay, tell the person to stop immediately. If the person persists, walk or run away.

This may seem like a harsh conversation for a ten- or twelve-year-old, but there are very young girls having babies and very young boys being molested. There are a lot of child molesters out there. The only way to instruct your children is to talk to them and listen to what they're telling you.

Teens

It is unlikely that your child will be completely honest about how much he or she has experienced sexually. They are much more likely at this age to get information and guidance from peers. This should not stop you from continuing to educate them. They may pretend not to be listening, they may never admit to reading the pamphlet on date rape that you left in their room, but do it anyway. Continue to build their self-esteem. Reward and encourage them to respect other people's feelings. You may not be comfortable saying to your son, "If you cross this line, it is rape." You may not be comfortable saying to your daughter, "If you are about to be raped by someone you know, this is what you should do." But you must say the words. Educating your children often and early is the best way to effectively combat date rape.

False reporting of a rape must also be discussed. Crying wolf to gain attention or for revenge is a dangerous ploy and has a devastating impact on the way true rape victims are treated.

During these talks, you are likely to get sighs of boredom, rolling eyes, and indignation from your teens, but stay with it. If they can't use it now, they will probably need it later.

Parking. Whether you want them to or not, it is likely that your children will go "parking" with a member of the opposite sex when they begin to date. While you may feel that this is inappropriate behavior, you should offer these guidelines "in case."

Make your intentions clear. Both teens should state clearly what they intend to do once they park. They should know what to expect from each other *before* they park. While this is likely to momentarily spoil the ambiance of the evening, it is likely to eliminate misunderstandings that could lead to rape. If one teen is uncomfortable about being straightforward or mocks your child for being so matter-of-fact about it, this is a good indication that this person is not emotionally mature enough to handle "parking" yet. It's time to go home.

Rapists. Rapists will stalk a known lovers lane and attack parkers, assaulting the male and raping the female. Teens appear to be easy, vulnerable targets for the rapist. For this reason, windows should be up, doors should be locked, and the teens should not leave the safety of the vehicle.

College Students

Sending your children off to college is a stressful and emotional time for everyone. There are so many other considerations that personal safety is likely to get lost in the shuffle. Freshmen and sophomore undergraduates are at the highest risk of becoming a victim of violent crime. They are in a new environment, they are governed by very few rules, and they are anxious to fit in. All of these things make them vulnerable.

Current studies indicate that one in four college students will be the victim of a sexual assault. Protect your college students by planting a few prevention seeds on their way out the door. The difference between consensual sex and rape should be discussed again with both young men and young women.

Review the facts:

1. Most victims of campus rape know their attackers.

2. Very often, alcohol is involved. If they decide to drink, it should be done in moderation and with a partner or one member of their group that agrees to stay sober.

3. Do not enter bathrooms alone at floor or frat house parties. Do not wander to another part of the house or grounds where there are fewer people.

4. Always lock dormitory doors. Individual rooms should have locks. If they do not, purchase a travel lock for your student to use.

5. Do not walk alone on campus. Travel in groups or pairs. If you find yourself having to cross campus after a late class alone, summon a security person for an escort. That is one of their functions.

6. Do not party with people you do not know.

7. Review the information on date rape prevention and self defense in this book.

8. Ask the college or university how they combat the problem of crime on campus. Ask if they offer personal safety awareness classes. Find out how many campus police officers they employ and if it is a 24 hour operation. Ask them to supply you with a crime report for the previous year.

9. When dating someone new, plan to double date with a friend for the first few dates.

The following is an exerpt taken from the "Teen Acquaintance Rape: A Community Response Project" in Seattle, Washington. I believe that the results of this survey, which was taken in 1980, will give you an idea of the attitudes that your high school and college students are up against.

This indicates the percentage of high school and college students saying it is acceptable for a male to hold a female down and force her to engage in intercourse under various conditions.

CONDITIONS	HIGH SCHOOL		COLLEGE	
	MALE	FEMALE	MALE	FEMALE
He spends a lot of money on her.	39%	12%	13%	8%
She is drunk.	39%	18%	21%	6%
She has led him on.	54%	26%	42%	28%
She changes her mind.	54%	31%	40%	22%
They have dated a long time.	43%	32%	42%	17%

The response from both males and females is disturbing.

Review
Preschoolers
—Know name, address and phone number.
—How to identify authority figures.
—Telephone—emergency number.
—Do not send them into public restrooms alone.
—Roll play stranger contact.
—Research molestation prevention.

Preteens
—Drug prevention.
—Rape prevention—boys and girls.

Teens
—Rape prevention—young men and young ladies.
—Parking.

College students
—Rape prevention—men and women.
—Check college crime.
—Discourage coed dormitories.
—Safety in numbers.
—Dorm room.

10

TEST YOUR PERSONAL SAFETY SKILLS

Here is a test of your personal safety skills. Take it and see if some of your views have changed. Consider the new knowledge that you have acquired and how you plan to react in the future.

1. Which statement most accurately reflects how you feel about violent crime?
   A. Crime is inevitable, I cannot change that.
   B. Why should I stay cooped up when the criminals can walk freely? I do what I want, when I want.
   C. I do as much as I can to reduce my risk of becoming a victim of violent crime.
   D. I have never really given it much thought.

2. Which statement best describes your actions in a parking lot?
   A. I wait and watch before I enter the lot.
   B. I have my keys out before I get to my car.
   C. I have a plan, in the event I am attacked.
   D. All of the above.
   E. None of the above.

3. Which statement best describes your lifestyle.
   A. I am single and spend a lot of time alone.
   B. I often go out at night to have a drink and be around other people.
   C. I usually walk most everywhere I go.
   D. I have a very active life and am constantly on the go.

4. Do you think that your lifestyle can have an effect on your odds of becoming a victim of violent crime?
   A. No
   B. Yes
   C. I have never really thought about it.

5. How do you carry your purse?
   A. With the strap over my shoulder.
   B. With the strap draped over my head and across my body.
   C. With the strap wrapped around my wrist.
   D. I carry a clutch bag in my hand.

6. If someone tried to rob you on the street, what would you do?
   A. I would cooperate.
   B. I would cooperate only if the robber had a weapon.
   C. I would fight for what is rightfully mine.

7. Do you feel your home is safe from intruders?
   A. Yes
   B. No

8. What steps have you taken to insure your safety at home?
   A. I have upgraded the locks on my doors and windows.
   B. I have a dog.
   C. I have an alarm system.
   D. No one has ever broken in, so I have never considered making any changes.

9. If you ever came home and found that your home had been burglarized, what would you do first?
   A. I would make a list of what is missing and call the police.
   B. I would leave the house, then go to a phone to call the police.
   C. I have no idea what I would do.

10. If you keep a gun in your home for safety, do you . . .
    A. Store the gun in one place and the ammo in another.
    B. Practice firing it regularly.
    C. Know when you can use deadly force.
    D. All of the above.
    E. None of the above.

11. When you are traveling in your vehicle, do you keep the doors locked and the windows rolled up?
    A. Yes, most of the time.
    B. Yes, sometimes.
    C. No.

12. If your vehicle broke down on an interstate and you were relatively close to an exit ramp, what would you do?
    A. Walk to a service station to get help.
    B. Flag someone down and ask for assistance.
    C. Wait for a police officer.
    D. I do not know what I would do.

13. If you were pulled over by someone in plainclothes who claimed to be a police officer, would you know how to determine whether the person was an imposter or an officer?
    A. Yes
    B. No

14. If you were attacked and about to be raped, what would you do?
    A. Fight and do whatever I could to get away. I would rather die than be raped.

B. I would scream and hope that someone would help.
C. Use my mace or another weapon that I carry.
D. My reaction would depend largely on the circumstances surrounding the attack.
E. I have never considered how I would handle it.

15. Which of these statements do you believe is most accurate about rape?
A. Most rapes occur at night, on the streets.
B. Most rapists are strangers, unknown to the victim.
C. Most rapists are known by their victims.
D. Most rapists are insane.

16. If you have children, have you discussed personal safety with them?
A. My children are still too young to understand.
B. I have taught them not to talk to strangers.
C. I do not want to frighten them, so I have not discussed it with them.Instead, I keep a close watch on them.
D. My children are old enough to know about these things. I do not see a need to discuss it with them further.

Let's review your responses.

Question 1 C—"I do as much as I can to reduce my risk of becoming a victim of violent crime," would be the desired response.

"As much as you can," means within reason, of course. You need to accept some responsibility for keeping yourself safe from violent crime. Take what action you can take, when you can take it.

Question 2 D—All of the above. Watch and wait before you enter a parking lot. Keep your door key in your hand and have a plan.

Question 3 Evaluate your lifestyle.

Question 4 B—Yes, your lifestyle can effect your odds of becoming a victim of violent crime. This does not mean that you have to severely alter your lifestyle, it simply means that you have to be aware that you could be in a high risk group.

Question 5 A—"Over the shoulder." The purse should be carried over the shoulder or in the hand so that you will not become entangled if someone tries to take it from you.

Question 6 A—"I would cooperate." In a robbery situation, offer resistance only to protect life—not to protect property.

Question 7 If the knowledge you have acquired has changed your mind about whether or not your home is safe, make the necessary changes.

Question 8 If your answer was "D", you need to have an assessment made of your home security. Do not wait for crime to strike before you decide to take steps to prevent it.

Question 9 B—"Yes, I would leave and go to a phone to call the police," is the desired response. If you walk in on a burglar, your personal safety could be in jeopardy.

Question 10 D—All of the above. If you decide to keep a gun in your home you should store it properly, practice regularly, and observe the statutory requirements for the use of deadly force.

Question 11 A—"Yes, most of the time." When in your vehicle, windows should be up and doors should be locked.

Question 12 C—"I would wait in my vehicle until the police arrived." You should wait for the police or someone you know. You should not leave the safety of your vehicle.

Question 13 You now have the information necessary to assist you in distinguishing an imposter from a police officer.

Question 14 D—"My reaction would depend largely on the circumstances surrounding the attack." Only you will possess all of the information necessary in an attack situation to choose the option that will enable you to survive.

Question 15 You know now that you cannot count on a rapist to match the image that you may have of him. He could be anyone. He could strike at anytime. You must be prepared for anything.

Question 16 B—Talking to your children about strangers is a start, but it is not enough. By now you know that you have to do some evaluating where your children are concerned and provide them with the information that they will need to stay safe.

CONCLUSION

It is my sincere hope that this book has made you more aware of the risk of becoming a victim of violent crime and more confident in your ability to deal with that risk. The decisions that you make will promote prevention and survival. You are on your own now.

Don't be scared. Be prepared.